PROGRAM ADMINISTRATION SCALE

THIRD EDITION

MEASURING WHOLE LEADERSHIP IN EARLY CHILDHOOD CENTERS

T0355127

Teri N. Talan, Ed.D., J.D. • Jill M. Bella, Ed.D. • Paula Jorde Bloom, Ph.D.

TEACHERS COLLEGE PRESS
TEACHERS COLLEGE | COLUMBIA UNIVERSITY
NEW YORK AND LONDON

Published by Teachers College Press,® 1234 Amsterdam Avenue, New York, NY 10027

Copyright © 2022 Teri N. Talan, Jill M. Bella, and Paula Jorde Bloom.

Front cover and title page images (left to right): PeopleImages via iStock by Getty Images, Zoran Zeremski via Shutterstock, and fizkes via iStock by Getty Images.

PAS® and Program Administration Scale® are registered trademarks of Teachers College, Columbia University.

ISBN 978-0-8077-6760-3

Printed on acid-free paper
Manufactured in the United States of America

2 3 4 5 6 7 8 9 10

Contact Dr. Teri N. Talan at teri.talan@nl.edu or Dr. Jill Bella at bellamattinaconsulting@gmail.com for further information.

Contents

Contents

Acknowledgments

Since the publication of the first edition of the *Program Administration Scale* (PAS) in 2004, we have had the privilege of working with thousands of early childhood administrators, technical assistance specialists, and policymakers across the United States, Canada, China, and Singapore. Some of these individuals attended intensive assessor reliability training and became certified PAS assessors so they could collect data for research or quality improvement initiatives. We are so appreciative of the clarifying questions and insightful comments we received at each of these training events. We want to express our gratitude to all the training participants and acknowledge their valuable contribution to this third edition of the *Program Administration Scale*.

The impetus for the PAS came from our work assessing program quality as part of a McCormick Foundation professional development initiative. The experience convinced us of the need for a valid and reliable instrument to measure the quality of administrative practices of center-based early care and education programs. The W. Clement and Jessie V. Stone Foundation provided the funding to conduct the initial reliability and validity study of the PAS. We are indebted to both foundations for their continuing commitment to improving the quality of early childhood program administration.

We are also grateful for the insights we received from experts in the field who helped shape the development of the *Program Administration Scale*. Our heartfelt thanks go to Kay Albrecht, Bee Jay Ciszek, Doug Clark, Dick Clifford, Debby Cryer, Eileen Eisenberg, Jana Fleming, Lois Gamble, John Gunnarson, Thelma Harms, Judy Harris Helm, Kendra Kett, Stacy Kim, Jackie Legg, Sam Meisels, Anne Mitchell, Gwen Morgan, Kathie Raiborn, Susan Sponheimer, Marilyn Sprague-Smith, and Lana Weiner. We also benefited from our discussions with the National Association for the Education of Young Children (NAEYC) Program Administration Standards Technical Review Team under the leadership of Stacie Goffin, Linda Espinosa, and Barbara Smith.

Appreciation also goes to the research team involved in our initial reliability and validity study of the PAS—Linda Butkovich, Lisa Downey, Shirley Flath, Kathryn Hardy, Karen May, Gale Reinitz, Sara Starbuck, and Cass Wolfe. The staff at the Illinois Network of Child Care Resource and Referral Agencies (INCCRRA) and the Metropolitan Chicago Information Center (MCIC) were particularly helpful during the sample selection process for our initial reliability study.

We also want to recognize the certified PAS assessors who conducted the PAS assessments in 31 states and the District of Columbia that were used in the national reliability and validity study reported in this third edition of the PAS. These valued colleagues are too numerous to name, but without their important contributions, the development of updated national norms would not have been possible.

We are extremely grateful for the statistical support we received from Robyn Kelton. Her assistance with coding and analyzing the data from our national sample saved us considerable time. Thanks as well to Lindsey Engelhardt, who did the layout of the final document, and Linda Butkovich, who provided a critical eye in proofing the content.

It has been a real pleasure to work with the editors and production team at Teachers College Press. Our deep appreciation to Sarah Biondello for keeping us focused and navigating this project through the production line.

And finally, members of the PAS Review Team at the McCormick Center for Early Childhood Leadership merit special recognition— Linda Butkovich, Robyn Kelton, Shuntae Richardson, and Paula Steffen. Their tireless efforts in responding to questions from the field, supporting end users, and overseeing our PAS certification system provided the foundation for the refinements in this third edition. Their expertise about the nuances of the PAS is invaluable to our work.

About the Authors

Teri N. Talan, Ed.D., J.D.

Teri N. Talan is the Michael W. Louis Chair and Senior Policy Advisor for the McCormick Center for Early Childhood Leadership and Professor of Early Childhood Education at National Louis University in Chicago, Illinois. She represents the McCormick Center in public policy forums and promotes action by local, state, and national policymakers on early childhood education and program administration issues. She is also the editor of the McCormick Center's quarterly *Research Notes*. Previously, Dr. Talan was the Executive Director of a NAEYC-accredited early childhood program. She holds a law degree from Northwestern University as well as a doctorate in Adult and Continuing Education and a graduate degree in Early Childhood Leadership and Advocacy from National Louis University. Dr. Talan's research interests are in the areas of early childhood leadership, workforce development, systems integration, and program quality evaluation. In addition to the *Program Administration Scale*, she is co-author of the *Business Administration Scale for Family Child Care* (BAS); *Escala de Evaluación de la Administración de Negocios*; *Building on Whole Leadership*; and the reports *Who's Caring for the Kids? The Status of the Early Childhood Workforce in Illinois* and *Closing the Leadership Gap*.

Jill M. Bella, Ed.D.

Dr. Jill M. Bella of Bella Mattina provides consultation and training to local and state initiatives focused on leadership topics in early care and education. She holds a doctorate in Adult and Continuing Education from National Louis University (NLU), and both a graduate degree in Special Education—Early Intervention and a baccalaureate degree in Child Development from the University of Illinois at Urbana-Champaign. Previously, Dr. Bella was Director of Professional Learning and an Assistant Professor at the McCormick Center for Early Childhood Leadership at NLU. In this role, she consulted on leadership initiatives, oversaw work on several assessment tools, designed and delivered trainings, and conducted research. Dr. Bella also worked as an early interventionist, training specialist, and early educator. Her interests include organizational climate, the early childhood workforce, systems thinking, and early childhood leadership. She is co-author of the *Program Administration Scale; A Great Place to Work; Building Whole Leadership; Inspiring Peak Performance; Zoom: The Impact of Early Childhood Leadership Training on Role Perceptions, Job Performance, and Career Decisions*; and several trainer's guides in the Director's Toolbox Management Series.

Paula Jorde Bloom, Ph.D. (d. 2018)

Paula Jorde Bloom was the founder and first Executive Director of the McCormick Center for Early Childhood Leadership as well as Emerita Professor of Early Childhood Education at National Louis University. As one of the country's leading experts on early childhood leadership and program administration issues, Dr. Bloom was a frequent keynote speaker at state, national, and international conferences and consultant to professional organizations and state agencies. She received her graduate and doctoral degrees from Stanford University. She authored numerous journal articles and widely read books, including *Avoiding Burnout; Blueprint for Action; Circle of Influence; Making the Most of Meetings; Workshop Essentials; Measuring Work Attitudes; From the Inside Out*; and *Leadership in Action*. Dr. Bloom created the *Early Childhood Work Environment Survey* (ECWES) and the *Early Childhood Job Satisfaction Survey* (ECJSS). Her influence lives on in the *Program Administration Scale*'s third edition.

Preface to the Third Edition

In the ten years since the second edition of the PAS was published, the body of research highlighting the importance of effective leadership practices in early childhood settings has greatly increased (Abel, Talan, & Masterson, 2017; Aubrey, Godfrey, & Harris, 2012; Bassok, Bellows, Markowitz, & Sadowski, 2021; Bloom & Abel, 2015; Bloom, Hentschel, & Bella, 2013; Caven, Khanani, Zhang, & Parker, 2021; Dennis & O'Connor, 2013; Douglass, 2017; Douglass, 2018; Gittell, 2016; Hewett & La Paro, 2020; Hujala et al., 2016; Institute of Medicine & National Research Council, 2015; Kangas, Venninen, & Ojala, 2015; King et al., 2015; Kirby et al., 2021; McCormick Center for Early Childhood Leadership, 2021; Minkos et. al., 2017; Whalen, Horsley, Parkinson, & Pacchiano, 2016; Zeng, Douglass, Lee, & DelVecchio, 2020; Zinsser, Denham, Curby, & Chazan-Cohen, 2016).

Several empirical studies have also been conducted that underscore the usefulness of the PAS as a reliable tool for measuring, monitoring, and improving administrative practices (Arend, 2010; Bloom & Talan, 2006; Derrick-Mills et al., 2016; Doherty, Ferguson, Ressler, & Lomotey, 2015; Etters & Capizzano, 2016; Kagan et al., 2008; MCECL, 2010; McKelvey et al., 2010; Mietlicki, 2010; Miller & Bogatova, 2007; Rous et al., 2008; Talan, Bloom, & Kelton, 2014; Yaya-Bryson, Scott-Little, Akman, & Cassidy, 2020).

Concurrently, the PAS has been found to be a useful tool in state quality rating and improvement systems and in the self-study process for programs seeking NAEYC center accreditation (Means & Pepper, 2010; Stephens, 2009). The rubrics for each indicator strand provide a convenient way for early childhood administrators to benchmark incremental change in the quality of their administrative practices.

While the review of current research did not suggest a need for a major revision of the PAS, there was an urgent need to respond to two recent societal developments impacting the field of early care and education. The first is an equity and social justice reckoning, and the second is the workforce crisis that threatens not only the early care and education field but the economy of United States as a whole. The PAS indicator language was reviewed from a racial equity and social justice perspective, and revisions were made resulting from this review. The workforce crisis has reinforced the need for administrative leadership practices that address compensation parity based on comparable qualifications regardless of the program's funding source or the age of the children served. Workforce supports that promote teacher leadership, enhance career development, and protect time for reflection, planning, and peer learning are critical aspects of effective program leadership.

The third edition of the PAS provides an opportunity to share updated information supporting the reliability and validity of the instrument. To some degree, the PAS has been "under construction" since it was first published in 2004. Practitioners using the PAS have asked probing questions about the indicators of administrative quality and provided insightful commentary about each of the PAS items. They have cast a bright light on how the PAS measures and supports administrative quality in a variety of program contexts. These practitioners, from across the country and representing all sectors of our field, have used the PAS for program self-improvement, research, training, college instruction, accreditation facilitation, quality monitoring, mentoring, coaching, organizational consulting, and policymaking. Based on the feedback from this wide range of stakeholders, extensive additional notes have been developed to support the reliable use of the PAS to assess administrative practices in the rich variety of program contexts that define our field.

Although the additional notes have been available electronically, they have been used primarily by those attending PAS reliability training. The additional notes are now embedded in this third edition of the PAS. As a result, program directors using the PAS for self-assessment, as well as those trained to reliably use the PAS for research, quality monitoring, or program support, will be able to rate the PAS indicators more accurately.

An additional goal for this third edition was to update the PAS to reflect changes in the early childhood field as well as incorporate new, evidence-based information relating to administrative quality. As a result, refinements to the PAS have been made.

- ◆ The PAS measures whole leadership in three domains of administrative practice—leadership essentials, administrative leadership, and pedagogical leadership.

- ◆ Subscales and items have been reorganized to better represent whole leadership functions.

- ◆ Competency areas aligned with each domain of whole leadership practice are addressed in Item 22, Administrator Qualifications.

- ◆ Administrative intensity is acknowledged as an element of quality, with staffing allocation for pedagogical leadership functions based on the number of classrooms within a center.

- ◆ A greater emphasis is placed on leadership practices that support inclusion, equity, and cultural and linguistic diversity.

- ◆ There is a new focus on leadership routines that provide opportunities for shared decision-making and distributed leadership among staff.

- ◆ There is attention placed on technology practices that promote information security.

- ◆ Embedded practices that promote continuous quality improvement are measured at both the classroom and organizational levels.

Finally, several changes were made to the structure of the third edition to increase user-friendliness: Indicator strands were reorganized, the asterisks connecting indicator language with an explanation in the Notes were replaced with a lettering system, and the Notes for each of the PAS items have been expanded to increase understanding and facilitate greater consistency in completing the PAS by all users.

Overview of the Program Administration Scale

Rationale

The genesis of the *Program Administration Scale* (PAS) was the growing professional consensus that early childhood program quality should to be viewed through a broader lens than only the classroom learning environment. Without quality systems in place at the organizational level, high-quality interactions and learning environments at the classroom level cannot be sustained. While there were several instruments available to measure the quality of teacher-child interactions and the quality of the classroom instructional practices, until the development of the PAS there did not exist a valid and reliable instrument that solely measured the administrative practices of early childhood programs.

The instrument includes 25 items clustered in 9 subscales that measure whole leadership functions of center-based early childhood programs. Whole leadership encompasses a broad view of program leadership—evidenced in many areas and organized into three domains:

- *Leadership essentials* refers to the foundational competencies necessary for leading people that are expressed in personal leadership behaviors. Leadership essentials are often developed through reflective practice and include cultural competence and relational leadership.
- *Pedagogical leadership* refers to facilitating the art and science of teaching with an emphasis on ensuring high quality interactions with children. Pedagogical leadership also includes fidelity to curricular philosophy, assessing children's development and learning, using data for evaluation, and optimizing learning environments.
- *Administrative leadership* refers to competencies necessary for organizational stability and growth. Administrative leadership practices include systems development, strategic planning, operational oversight, advocacy, and community collaboration.

The McCormick Center for Early Childhood Leadership at National Louis University developed the Whole Leadership Framework in order to clarify the core areas of early childhood leadership, which is often clouded by inconsistent state standards and policies (Abel, Talan, & Masterson, 2017).

Designed for early childhood program administrators, researchers, monitoring personnel, and quality enhancement facilitators, the PAS was constructed to complement the widely used Environment Rating Scales developed by Harms, Clifford, and Cryer. Both the PAS and the Environment Rating Scales measure quality on a 7-point scale, and both generate a profile to guide program improvement efforts. If used together, these instruments provide a focused look at effective practices at the classroom level and the broad view of program quality from an organizational perspective (Kagan, et al., 2008; McKelvey, et al., 2010).

Multi-Use Design

The *Program Administration Scale* is applicable for multiple uses: program self-improvement, technical assistance and monitoring, training, research and evaluation, and public awareness. The target audience for the PAS is center-based early childhood programs including Head Start and state-funded pre-K programs.

- **Program self-improvement.** Because indicators are objective and quantifiable on a 7-point continuum from inadequate to excellent, program administrators can easily set program goals to incrementally improve administrative practices. The resulting profile can be used to benchmark a center's progress in meeting those goals over time.

- **Technical assistance and monitoring.** As part of local or state quality-enhancement initiatives, the PAS can serve as a convenient technical assistance and monitoring tool providing clear guidelines for incrementally improving organizational practices to ensure high-quality programming for children and families.

- **Training.** For both pre-service and in-service training for program administrators, the PAS provides a broad overview of organizational practices, highlights effective practices in whole leadership, and reinforces the important role that program administrators play in shaping program quality.

- **Research and evaluation.** For independent research studies or publicly funded quality rating and improvement systems (QRIS) that reward higher levels of program quality, the PAS can be used to describe current levels of program quality as well as benchmark change in pretest–posttest evaluation designs.

- **Public awareness.** Because the PAS is written in clear language and provides a rubric of concrete examples of whole leadership practices, it can help inform a wide range of key constituents—program administrative staff, state policymakers, licensing representatives, families, and technical assistance specialists—about the components of high-quality programming.

Subscales, Items, and Indicators

As explained earlier, the PAS measures quality on a 7-point scale in 25 items clustered in 9 subscales. The first 23 items relate to all programs. The last two items (Item 24 Teacher and Item 25 Assistant Teacher/ Aide) are optional items depending on the program's staffing pattern. Each item is comprised of 2–5 indicator strands, and each indicator strand is scored on a 7-point scale from inadequate to excellent.

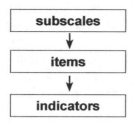

The following is a description of the subscales into which the items are grouped:

- **Human Resources** assesses hiring and orientation components, performance appraisal criteria and processes, and professional development requirements and supports.

- **Personnel Cost and Allocation** looks at whether the organization has a written salary scale and annual salary increases, the type and availability of fringe benefits, whether children are regrouped during the day to maintain ratios, the availability of paid planning time for teaching staff, and staffing for pedagogical leadership.

- **Operations** considers routine maintenance of the facility, the adequacy of the space to meet the needs of staff, whether the center has a risk management plan and what it includes, public relations tools, and the use of technology, including security practices.

- **Screening and Assessment** examines screening procedures to assist in the identification of children with disabilities, practices that promote collaboration with specialists, measures to assess and analyze children's learning and developmental outcomes, and whether the results of child assessments are used in lesson planning and plan, do, study, act cycles of quality improvement.

- **Fiscal Management** looks at the director's involvement with the annual budget planning process, line item breakdowns, if payroll and other expenses are paid in a timely manner, whether the center has accounting checks and balances in place, and if standard accounting procedures are adhered to.

- **Organizational Growth and Development** assesses whether the center utilizes a written mission and vision statement, engages in strategic planning, uses tools to measure teaching, learning, and overall program quality, and makes decisions based on evaluation and feedback.

- **Family and Community Partnerships** examines family orientation practices and conferencing options; the type and frequency of communication with families; family supports offered; the level of family engagement in center events, classroom routines, and decision-making; how responsive the center is to the needs of the neighborhood or local community; and staff involvement in early childhood professional organizations, as well as local civic, business, or faith-based organizations.

- **Relational Leadership** evaluates the components of staff meetings, inclusive leadership practices, opportunities for staff to reflect on personal biases and review professional practices, and conflict resolution supports.

- **Staff Qualifications** considers the level of general education, specialized training, and work experience of the Administrator and members of the teaching staff.

Definition of Terms

The following definitions are used consistently throughout the PAS and should be used in completing the PAS.

Administrative staff	A member of the administrative team, typically someone in a supervisory role. May include director, assistant director, or coordinator.
Administrator	The individual who has primary responsibility for planning, implementing, and evaluating the early childhood program. The Administrator must be located on-site if the center has four or more classrooms or a total enrollment of 60 or more full-time equivalent (FTE) children. Role titles for the Administrator vary and may include director, manager, coordinator, or principal.
Assistant Teacher/ Aide	A member of the teaching team assigned to a group of children who works under the direct supervision of the Lead Teacher and/or Teacher.
CDA	Child Development Associate® Credential.
Center/Program	Unit of analysis for completing the PAS.
ECE/CD	Early childhood education or child development.
Employees/Staff	More than one individual paid to perform administrative, teaching, and/or support functions.

Family	Includes parents or guardians.
FTE	Full-time equivalent.
Lead Teacher	The individual with the highest professional qualifications assigned to teach a group of children and who is responsible for daily lesson planning, family conferences, child assessment, and curriculum planning. This individual may also supervise other members of the teaching team. Role titles for the Lead Teacher vary and may include head teacher, master teacher, or teacher.
Plan-do-study-act cycle	An iterative process for quality improvement that includes making a plan, implementing the plan, reflecting on accomplishments and any changes needed, and determining the steps for the next cycle of plan-do-study-act (e.g., plan-do-review; rapid cycle improvement).
sh	Semester hours of college credit.
Support staff	Individuals who support the work of administrative and/or teaching staff as well as center operations. May include kitchen, transportation, clerical, and maintenance staff.
Teacher	A member of the teaching team who shares responsibility with the Lead Teacher for the care and education of an assigned group of children.
Teaching staff	Includes Lead Teachers, Teachers, and/or Assistant Teachers/Aides.
Whole Leadership Framework	Encompasses a broad view of program leadership—evidenced in many areas and organized into three domains: leadership essentials, administrative leadership, and pedagogical leadership. Whole leadership reflects an interdependent relationship between the three leadership domains.

Using the Program Administration Scale

Data-Collection Procedures

The *Program Administration Scale* was designed for use by program administrators as well as by trained independent assessors such as researchers, consultants, or program evaluators. The independent assessor using the PAS should schedule approximately three hours for an interview with the Administrator and an additional three hours for a review of documents. In advance of the visit, it is recommended that the Administrator be provided with a copy of the PAS and the Documents for Review form, which is available on the McCormick Center's website (McCormickCenter.nl.edu).

Upon arriving for the interview, the assessor should first ask the Administrator for a brief tour of the facility, including any space specifically designated for families and staff. Observations of the facility are needed to complete the scoring of three items (Item 7 Facilities, Item 8 Risk Management, and Item 15, Strategic Planning). For the indicators needing documentation, the assessor should record a preliminary rating based on statements made by the Administrator during the interview. After the interview, a thorough review of the documents should be conducted and adjustments made to the rating of the indicators if necessary.

Rating and Scoring

Adhering to the following two scoring principles for the *Program Administration Scale* will ensure the accuracy of the PAS profile and promote consistency in scoring across programs.

- In order to provide an accurate snapshot of whole leadership practices, it is important that ratings be based only on the indicators provided for each item. For some indicators, ratings are based solely on the Administrator's self-report

(e.g., Item 2 Supervision and Performance Appraisal, Indicator 3.3). However, for most indicators, it is necessary to review documents or make observations in order to verify the accuracy of the information provided by the Administrator. **For these verifiable indicators, a "D" (document) or an "O" (observation) appears under the indicator number** (e.g., Item 15 Strategic Planning, Indicator 5.2).

- Scores should be based on existing and current policies and procedures, not past practices or plans for the future. A practice is considered current if it has happened within the past 12 months of the date of the assessment.

The following protocol should be used to score the *Program Administration Scale*:

Step 1. Rate the indicators for Items 1–21.
Use the following rules for rating the indicators:

- For each item, begin with the indicator under the 1 (inadequate) category and proceed across the continuum of quality for each indicator to 7 (excellent), writing in the spaces provided a Y (yes) or N (no). Proceed to the next row, continuing until all indicators in the item are rated.

- A rating of N/A (not applicable) may be given for indicators or for entire items when "N/A is allowed" is shown on the scale. Indicators rated N/A are not counted when determining the score for an item, and items scored N/A are not counted when calculating the Total PAS Score.

- Record notes or supporting evidence for each indicator in the empty space on each page (e.g., practice described meets the criteria specified or an observation is made).

- After rating all indicators for Items 1–21 and verifying documentation, record the rationale for any indicators where credit is not received in the space labeled *Rationale* at the bottom of each scale page.

Step 2. Determine the scores for Items 1–21.
Use the following scoring rules for determining the item scores:

- A score of 1 is given if any indicator under the 1 column is rated Y (yes). A score of 1 is also given if all indicators under the 1 column are rated N (no) and less than half of the indicators under the 3 column are rated Y (yes).

- A score of 2 is given when all indicators under 1 are rated N (no) and at least half of the indicators under 3 are rated Y (yes).

- A score of 3 is given when all indicators under 1 are rated N (no) and all indicators under 3 are rated Y (yes).

- A score of 4 is given when all indicators under 1 are rated N (no), all indicators under 3 are rated Y (yes), and at least half of the indicators under 5 are rated Y (yes).

- A score of 5 is given when all indicators under 1 are rated N (no), and all indicators under 3 and 5 are rated Y (yes).

- A score of 6 is given when all indicators under 1 are rated N (no), all the indicators under 3 and 5 are rated Y (yes), and at least half of the indicators under 7 are rated Y (yes).

- A score of 7 is given when all indicators under 1 are rated N (no) and all indicators under 3, 5, and 7 are rated Y (yes).

Circle the item score in the space provided in the lower right-hand corner on each item page.

Step 3. Determine the scores for Items 22–25.
Complete the **Administrator Qualifications Worksheet** (page 62). Only one person is designated as the Administrator.

- Use this information to rate the indicators for Item 22 Administrator.
- Follow the scoring rules provided in Steps 1 and 2.

Complete a **Teaching Staff Qualifications Worksheet** (page 63) for each classroom/group of children, duplicating the form as needed.

- For completing the PAS, it is necessary to designate only one of the adults responsible for the care and education of an assigned group of children as the Lead Teacher. The Lead Teacher is the individual with the highest professional qualifications. When two or more teaching staff members in the same classroom/working with the same group of children meet this definition (e.g., share the exact same responsibilities, are co-teachers), select the individual with the highest professional qualifications and complete the Lead Teacher Item for this individual.

- Designate any other member of the teaching team who shares responsibility with the Lead Teacher for the care and education of an assigned group of children as a Teacher.

- Designate any member of the teaching team who works under the direct supervision of the Lead Teacher and/or Teacher as an Assistant Teacher/Aide.

- Not all centers will have a staffing pattern that includes Teachers and/or Assistant Teachers/Aides.

- Use the information from the **Teaching Staff Qualifications Worksheet** to rate the indicators for Item 23 Lead Teacher, Item 24 Teacher, and Item 25 Assistant Teacher/Aide.

- Duplicate sufficient copies of Items 23, 24, and 25 so that the qualifications of each member of the teaching staff can be rated separately.

- Follow the rules provided in Steps 1 and 2 to score the teaching staff qualification Items 23, 24, and 25.

Complete the **Summary of Teaching Staff Qualifications Worksheet** (page 64).

- Transfer the individual item scores for each member of the teaching staff to the **Summary of Teaching Staff Qualifications Worksheet.**

- Use the qualifications of the Lead Teachers assigned to each group of children to compute the Item 23 Average Score. Round this score to the closest whole number and enter on the **Item Summary** form (page 65) for Item 23.

- Use the qualifications of any Teachers assigned to each group of children to compute the Item 24 Average Score.

Round this score to the closest whole number and enter on the **PAS Item Summary** form for Item 24.

- Use the qualifications of any Assistant Teachers/Aides assigned to each group of children to compute the Item 25 Average Score. Round this score to the closest whole number and enter on the **PAS Item Summary** form for Item 25.

Step 4. Generate a Total PAS Score.
The Total PAS Score is the sum of the item scores. To calculate the Total PAS score, transfer the individual item scores to the **PAS Item Summary** form on page 65. Sum the item scores for the entire scale.

- If the program has a staffing pattern that includes both Teachers **and** Assistant Teachers/Aides, then 25 items are rated and scored.

- If the program has a staffing pattern that includes only Teachers **or only** Assistant Teachers/Aides, then 24 items are rated and scored.

- If the program has a staffing pattern that does **not** include Teachers **and** does not include Assistant Teachers/Aides, then 23 items are rated and scored.

- Note, if the program serves only school-aged children, items 11 and 12 will have a score of N/A.

Step 5. Determine the Average PAS Item Score.

Use the **PAS Item Summary** form to calculate the Average PAS Item Score, which is the Total PAS Score divided by the number of items scored (minimum of 21 for all programs; 22, 23, 24, or 25 depending on whether or not the program has scored items 11, 12, 24, and 25 as N/A).

Step 6. Plot scores on the PAS Profile.

Plot the individual item scores on the graph of the **PAS Profile** form on page 66; then connect the dots. Add the information at the bottom of the profile regarding the Total PAS Score, number of items scored, and Average PAS Item Score.

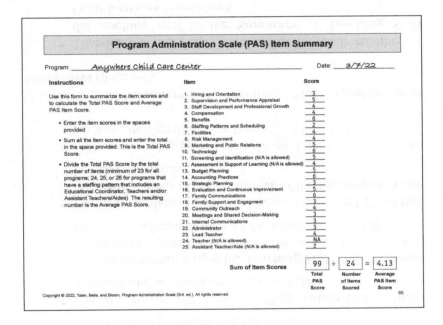

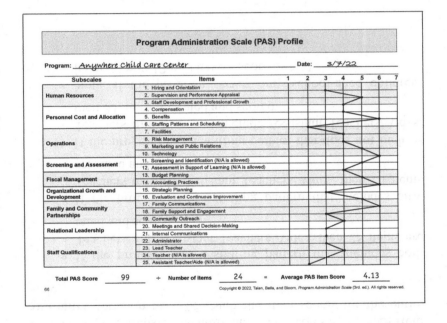

Program Administration Scale

Subscales and Items

Human Resources

1. Hiring and Orientation
2. Supervision and Performance Appraisal
3. Staff Development and Professional Growth

Personnel Cost and Allocation

4. Compensation
5. Benefits
6. Staffing Patterns and Scheduling

Operations

7. Facilities
8. Risk Management
9. Marketing and Public Relations
10. Technology

Screening and Assessment

11. Screening and Identification (N/A is Allowed)
12. Assessment in Support of Learning (N/A is Allowed)

Fiscal Management

13. Budget Planning
14. Accounting Practices

Organizational Growth and Development

15. Strategic Planning
16. Evaluation and Continuous Improvement

Family and Community Partnerships

17. Family Communications
18. Family Support and Engagement
19. Community Outreach

Relational Leadership

20. Meetings and Shared Decision-Making
21. Internal Communications

Staff Qualifications

22. Administrator
23. Lead Teacher
24. Teacher (N/A is Allowed)
25. Assistant Teacher/Aide (N/A is Allowed)

Human Resources

1. Hiring and Orientation

Notes

a Additional hiring practices **may** include:

- ❏ interview questions that comply with federal employment anti-discrimination laws and the Americans with Disabilities Act (ADA)
- ❏ interviewers complete an interview summary form prior to debriefing
- ❏ interviewers reflect the diversity of the children and families served
- ❏ multiple sources of evidence (e.g., classroom observation, portfolio review, reference check, review of professional development records, review of transcripts, teaching demonstration)
- ❏ personal benefits (e.g., health insurance, dental insurance, life insurance, vacation, sick leave, personal leave, parental leave, reduced child care cost, retirement plan) are communicated
- ❏ predetermined interview questions are used for each candidate in the same role
- ❏ professional benefits for teaching and administrative staff (e.g., membership in a professional organization, release time to visit other centers, tuition reimbursement, conference or workshop registration fee, paid release time for professional development/college course, subscription to professional journal, credential or certification fee, apprenticeship program) are communicated
- ❏ two or more staff are involved in the interviewing process
- ❏ two or more staff are included in the hiring decision
- ❏ other _____

b *Staff orientation* refers to a process that occurs after a new employee is hired, with a focus on supporting the new employee to effectively transition into the early childhood program and fulfill the responsibilities of the position.

c The orientation policy **must** be specific to the early childhood program but may also include the orientation procedures of a sponsoring agency.

The orientation policy/documents (e.g., orientation checklist) **must** include:

- ❏ a timeframe for the orientation process
- ❏ activities to occur during the orientation process
- ❏ personnel involved in the orientation process
- ❏ specific practices and procedures to be implemented by new staff (e.g., guidance and discipline, child abuse and neglect reporting)

d *A phased staff orientation* (sometimes referred to as *onboarding*) helps in the retention of new employees and takes place over a defined period of time. The phased orientation **must** include:

- ❏ Phase 1: introduction to the center staff, organizational norms, and sharing critical information
- ❏ Phase 2: skill-building, observation, feedback, and support
- ❏ Phase 3: goal-setting at the conclusion of probationary period

e The purpose of this feedback is to improve the phased staff orientation for future employees.

Human Resources

1. Hiring and Orientation

	1	2	3	4	5	6	7
	Inadequate		**Minimal**		**Good**		**Excellent**

___ 1.1 The hiring procedures do not include an interview, providing the job description, and at least two additional practices.[a]

___ 3.1 D The hiring procedures include an interview, providing the job description, and at least two additional practices.[a]

___ 5.1 D The hiring procedures include an interview, providing the job description, and at least four additional practices.[a]

___ 7.1 D The hiring procedures include an interview, providing the job description, and at least six additional practices.[a]

___ 1.2 There is no orientation for new staff.[b]

___ 3.2 D There is an orientation for new staff that includes receiving a copy of the staff handbook, personnel policies, and the family handbook.[b]

___ 5.2 D During the first week of employment the supervisor meets with the new employee to review and discuss the program mission/vision, job responsibilities, and policies and procedures.[b]

___ 7.2 D The orientation for new teaching staff includes a minimum of a half-day observation in their assigned classrooms prior to assuming responsibility for children.[b]

___ 1.3 There is no staff orientation policy.[b]

___ 3.3 D There is a staff orientation policy.[b,c]

___ 5.3 D The staff orientation policy has been reviewed within the last three years.[b,c]

___ 7.3 D The staff orientation policy is reviewed annually.[b,c]

___ 5.4 D A phased staff orientation is conducted throughout the introductory or probationary period for new staff.[b,d]

___ 7.4 D Written feedback about the phased staff orientation is obtained from newly hired staff after the conclusion of the introductory or probationary period.[b,d,e]

Rationale:

Circle the final score based on the scoring rules on pages 5–6.

1   2   3   4   5   6   7

1. Hiring and Orientation

2. Supervision and Performance Appraisal

Notes

This item is concerned with the supervision and performance appraisal of teaching staff only.

a   Goals for professional development **must** relate to the performance appraisal criteria and specify desired improvements in professional practice.

Professional development activities refers to specific learning strategies (e.g., college course, online training, workshop, observation by a mentor, observation of another teacher/classroom) planned to achieve identified goals.

b   *Teaching staff are formally observed* when the observation is conducted for the exclusive purpose of assessing and improving teaching practices.

c   A system to provide ongoing feedback and support to all teaching staff **must** include:

❑ tangible, concrete evidence _____

❑ involvement of multiple individuals _____

❑ a defined process of accountability _____

2. Supervision and Performance Appraisal

1	2	3	4	5	6	7
Inadequate		**Minimal**		**Good**		**Excellent**

___ 1.1 Performance appraisal is not conducted by the supervisor for all teaching staff (Lead Teachers, Teachers, and/or Assistant Teachers/Aides).

___ 3.1 D Performance appraisal is conducted by the supervisor for all teaching staff (Lead Teachers, Teachers, and/or Assistant Teachers/Aides).

___ 5.1 D All teaching staff (Lead Teachers, Teachers, and/or Assistant Teachers/Aides) participate in an annual performance appraisal process (e.g., complete a written self-appraisal, provide feedback on appraisal before it is finalized).

___ 7.1 D Annual performance appraisal for all teaching staff (Lead Teachers, Teachers, and/or Assistant Teachers/Aides) includes goals and professional development activities for the next year.[a]

___ 1.2 The criteria on the performance appraisal form are mostly subjective and trait-based (e.g., teacher is warm, friendly, and caring).

___ 3.2 D The criteria on the performance appraisal form are mostly objective and behavior-based (e.g., teacher uses positive guidance techniques, asks children open-ended questions).

___ 5.2 D The criteria on the performance appraisal form differ by role and are tied to the specific responsibilities detailed in each job description.

___ 7.2 D The performance appraisal process includes multiple sources of evidence (e.g., artifacts, parent feedback, co-worker feedback).

___ 1.3 Teaching staff are not formally observed as part of the supervision and performance appraisal process.[b]

___ 3.3 Teaching staff are formally observed as part of the supervision and performance appraisal process.[b]

___ 5.3 D At least three times a year, supervisors provide individual teaching staff or teaching teams with feedback based on formal observation of performance.

___ 7.3 D A system is implemented to provide feedback and support to all teaching staff at least monthly.[c]

Rationale:

Circle the final score based on the scoring rules on pages 5–6.

1   2   3   4   5   6   7

2. Supervision and Performance Appraisal

3. Staff Development and Professional Growth

Notes

a An individualized model of staff development **must** include:

❏ use of a form to identify an individual's specific learning needs based on their performance appraisal and goals

❏ an action plan to meet those needs with the following components: person responsible, specific activities to be completed, resources needed, timeline, and evaluation checkpoints

b A system to support the career development of teaching and administrative staff **must** include:

❏ tangible, concrete evidence _____

❏ involvement of multiple individuals _____

❏ a defined process of accountability _____

c *Job-embedded professional development* is defined as learning based on reflection and engagement grounded in daily teaching practice. Practices that support job-embedded professional development **may** include:

❏ a supervisor/coach who facilitates reflective activities and/ or provides additional resources as follow-up to professional development

❏ case studies used by teaching staff for critical analysis

❏ classroom or individual teaching staff observed by a supervisor/ coach to support teaching staff in making decisions to improve practice

❏ classroom portfolio that documents new learning applied in the classroom

❏ job description includes a responsibility related to professional growth that is assessed during the performance appraisal

❏ peer learning team that utilizes a protocol to guide quality improvement efforts

❏ supervision that supports teaching staff in reflecting-on-action, in-action, and/or for-action

❏ teaching staff who implement plan-do-study-act cycles to improve classroom quality

❏ teaching staff who observe one another and provide feedback

❏ teaching staff who engage in journaling that is utilized in reflective supervision

❏ teaching staff who share with peers how their teaching practices have been influenced by participation in professional development

❏ other _____

3. Staff Development and Professional Growth

1	2	3	4	5	6	7
Inadequate		**Minimal**		**Good**		**Excellent**

___ 1.1 Staff development for all administrative, teaching, and support staff is not available at no cost to staff.

___ 3.1 D Staff development for all administrative, teaching, and support staff is available at no cost to staff.

___ 5.1 D Job-specific staff development is provided for administrative, teaching, and support staff (e.g., administrators receive training on budgeting; teachers receive training on positive guidance; kitchen staff receive training on food sanitation).

___ 7.1 D Staff development for all administrative, teaching, and support staff on diversity, equity, and inclusion (e.g., anti-bias approaches to teaching, culturally responsive practices) is provided during orientation and minimally once per year thereafter.

___ 1.2 The program does not have a policy requiring all teaching and administrative staff to attend 15 or more clock hours of staff development each year **and** a professional development record is not maintained.

___ 3.2 D The program has a policy requiring all teaching and administrative staff to attend 15 or more clock hours of staff development each year **and** a professional development record is maintained.

___ 5.2 D The program has a policy requiring all teaching and administrative staff to attend 20 or more clock hours of staff development each year **and** a professional development record is maintained.

___ 7.2 D An individualized model of staff development is utilized for teaching and administrative staff.[a]

___ 1.3 Information regarding publicly funded professional development opportunities is not shared with staff on an ongoing basis.

___ 3.3 D Information regarding publicly funded professional development opportunities is shared with staff on an ongoing basis.

___ 5.3 D Staff are supported to advance on a career pathway (e.g., release time to attend classes or complete assignments, career advising).

___ 7.3 D A system exists to support the career development of teaching and administrative staff.[b]

___ 1.4 There are no practices that demonstrate job-embedded professional development for teaching staff.[c]

___ 3.4 D There are at least two practices that demonstrate job-embedded professional development for teaching staff.[c]

___ 5.4 D There are at least four practices that demonstrate job-embedded professional development for teaching staff.[c]

___ 7.4 D There are at least six practices that demonstrate job-embedded professional development for teaching staff.[c]

Rationale:

Circle the final score based on the scoring rules on pages 5–6.

1   2   3   4   5   6   7

3. Staff Development and Professional Growth

Personnel Cost and Allocation

4. Compensation

Notes

The salary scale must include all teaching roles at the center.

a   *Available* refers to unrestricted access to the salary scale that identifies the salary/wage ranges for new employees based on predetermined criteria.

b   *Internal equity* refers to the relationship between different jobs within an organization and is achieved through job analysis to determine the relative value or contribution of the work to the organization's goals. *External equity* refers to the relationship between similar jobs in the external labor market and is achieved by establishing the going rate for similar work performed by employees with similar qualifications.

c   *Education* refers to the level of general education (e.g., high school diploma, associate degree, baccalaureate degree). *Specialized training* refers to college coursework or other training specific to the role. *Professional credentials* refers to the certificates/licenses issued to early childhood practitioners by state agencies or national organizations in recognition of the achievement of professional competency.

d   A *merit increase* refers to an increase to the base salary. A bonus, unless it is an increase to the base salary, is not considered a merit increase.

Personnel Cost and Allocation

4. Compensation

	1	2	3	4	5	6	7
	Inadequate		**Minimal**		**Good**		**Excellent**

___ 1.1 A salary scale is not available to the Administrator.[a]

___ 3.1 D A salary scale is available to some center employees.[a]

___ 5.1 D A salary scale is available to all center employees.[a]

___ 7.1 D The salary scale was reviewed at least twice within the last five years for internal **and** external equity.[b]

___ 1.2 A salary scale is not differentiated by role and education.[c]

___ 3.2 D A salary scale is differentiated by role, education, and specialized training.[c]

___ 5.2 D A salary scale is differentiated by role, education, specialized training, and years of relevant experience.[c]

___ 7.2 D A salary scale is differentiated by role, education, specialized training, years of relevant experience, and professional credentials (e.g., infant-toddler, bilingual, administrator) or license (e.g., ECE I, II, III).[c]

___ 1.3 All employees (administrative, teaching, and support staff) did not receive a salary increase within the last two years.

___ 3.3 D All employees (administrative, teaching, and support staff) received a salary increase within the last two years.

___ 5.3 D All employees (administrative, teaching, and support staff) received a salary increase in each of the last three years.

___ 7.3 D The center has a compensation plan that provides for a merit increase in addition to an annual salary increase.[d]

Rationale:

Circle the final score based on the scoring rules on pages 5–6.

1   2   3   4   5   6   7

4. Compensation

5. Benefits

Notes

Employment terms:

All full-time employees refers to paid employees who work 35 or more hours per week unless the organization defines full-time employment differently as noted in the personnel policies or employee handbook.

All employees refers to full-time and part-time employees who work 20 or more hours per week. Work-study, seasonal, and part-time employees who work less than 20 hours per week are not included.

a   N/A is allowed only if there are no full-time employees.

b   Paid Time Off (PTO) includes paid holidays, vacation, and sick/personal leave.

c   The professional development benefit gives employees financial support to access professional development of their own choosing. Supervisor approval may be required. This benefit can be used for transportation, child care, or learning materials needed to participate in professional development.

5. Benefits

	1	2		3	4		5	6		7
	Inadequate			**Minimal**			**Good**			**Excellent**

___ 1.1 All full-time employees do not have the option to purchase health insurance with the employer paying a portion of the cost (N/A is allowed).[a]

___ 3.1 D All full-time employees have the option to purchase health insurance with the employer paying a portion of the cost (N/A is allowed).[a]

___ 5.1 D All full-time employees have the option to purchase health insurance with the employer paying 50% or more of the cost of the employee's coverage (N/A is allowed).[a]

___ 7.1 D All full-time employees have the option to purchase health insurance with the employer paying 66% or more of the cost of the employee's coverage (N/A is allowed).[a]

___ 1.2 All employees receive less than 11 days of PTO **during their first year** of employment.[b]

___ 3.2 D All employees receive 11 or more days of PTO **during their first year** of employment.[b]

___ 5.2 D All employees receive 19 or more days of PTO **during their first year** of employment.[b]

___ 7.2 D All employees receive 27 or more days of PTO **during their first year** of employment.[b]

___ 5.3 D All employees receive a minimum of 24 days of PTO **after completing their fifth year** of employment.[b]

___ 7.3 D All employees receive a minimum of 32 days of PTO **after completing their fifth year** of employment.[b]

___ 1.4 All full-time employees do not have the option of contributing to a retirement plan (N/A is allowed).[a]

___ 3.4 D All full-time employees have the option of contributing to a retirement plan (N/A is allowed).[a]

___ 5.4 D The employer matches 3% or more of the employee's salary contributed to a retirement plan (N/A is allowed).[a]

___ 7.4 D The employer matches 5% or more of the employee's salary contributed to a retirement plan (N/A is allowed).[a]

___ 1.5 The employer does not make any provision to pay for or reimburse professional development expenses.[c]

___ 3.5 D The employer makes some provision to pay for or reimburse professional development expenses.[c]

___ 5.5 D The employer provides $100 or more per year to all employees to pay for or reimburse professional development expenses.[c]

___ 7.5 D The employer provides $200 or more per year to all employees to pay for or reimburse professional development expenses.[c]

Rationale:

Circle the final score based on the scoring rules on pages 5–6.

1   2   3   4   5   6   7

5. Benefits

6. Staffing Patterns and Scheduling

Notes

a   *Regrouped to maintain required ratios* refers to when children are moved from one group to another because a member of the teaching team is absent, resulting in noncompliance with the required teacher-child ratio.

b   *Regrouped at the beginning or end of the day* refers to an intentional and consistent regrouping of children when a reduced number of children are present.

c   Paid planning and preparation time can occur during the children's nap time as long as it does not interfere with the adequate supervision of children.

d   *Pedagogical leadership* refers to the intentional practice of supporting, influencing, or guiding others to improve the quality of teaching and learning, as well as promoting partnerships with families and fostering family leadership in early care and education settings.

6. Staffing Patterns and Scheduling

	1	2	3	4	5	6	7
	Inadequate		**Minimal**		**Good**		**Excellent**

___ 1.1 Children are regrouped to maintain required ratios six or more times per year.[a]	___ 3.1 Children are regrouped to maintain required ratios less than six times per year.[a]

___ 5.1 D The staffing plan anticipates absences of teaching staff by providing "staffing over ratio" or a "floating teacher."

___ 7.1 D The staffing plan provides classroom coverage so that children are not regrouped at the beginning or end of the day.[b]

___ 1.2 There is no weekly paid planning or preparation time scheduled for teaching staff.[c]

___ 3.2 D There is weekly paid planning or preparation time scheduled for teaching staff.[c]

___ 5.2 D Paid curriculum planning time occurs at least every other week and includes all teaching staff working with the same group of children.

___ 7.2 D Teaching staff have the equivalent of at least 30 minutes of paid planning or preparation time per day that does not occur in the presence of children.

___ 1.3 In the center, two or more staff are not scheduled whenever children are present.

___ 3.3 D In the center, two or more staff are scheduled whenever children are present.

___ 5.3 D In each classroom, two or more teaching staff are scheduled whenever children are present including nap time (exception allowed during the first and last hour of operation).

___ 7.3 D In each classroom, two or more teaching staff are scheduled whenever children are present including nap time and the first and last hour of operation.

___ 1.4 The Administrator or a staff member does not have dedicated time and identified responsibilities for pedagogical leadership.[d]

___ 3.4 D The Administrator or a staff member has dedicated time and identified responsibilities for pedagogical leadership.[d]

___ 5.4 D There is a .5 FTE staff member with dedicated time and identified responsibilities for pedagogical leadership in centers with six or more classrooms or groups of children (N/A is allowed for programs with less than 6 classrooms or groups of children).[d]

___ 7.4 D There is a 1.0 FTE staff member with dedicated time and identified responsibilities for pedagogical leadership in centers with six or more classrooms or groups of children (N/A is allowed for programs with less than 6 classrooms or groups of children).[d]

Rationale:

Circle the final score based on the scoring rules on pages 5–6.

1   2   3   4   5   6   7

6. Staffing Patterns and Scheduling

Operations

7. Facilities

Notes

a   Examples of routine maintenance **may** include:

- ❏ contract for cleaning services
- ❏ contract for maintenance of heating and/or cooling system
- ❏ contract for pest control
- ❏ record of daily check of bathroom supplies and sanitation
- ❏ record of daily check of outdoor playground safety
- ❏ record of maintenance of alarm system
- ❏ record of maintenance of fire extinguisher and smoke detectors
- ❏ record of maintenance of playground equipment
- ❏ record of maintenance of ventilation system
- ❏ record of window cleaning
- ❏ other_____

b   Space that meets the individual needs of staff **must** include:

- ❏ an adult-sized chair or sofa in each classroom
- ❏ an enclosed storage area for personal belongings
- ❏ a separate adult restroom

c   *A professional library* **must** include:

- ❏ a computer with Internet access
- ❏ a minimum of 12 issues of a journal/magazine related to early childhood education
- ❏ a minimum of 25 books related to early childhood education

7. Facilities

1	2	3	4	5	6	7
Inadequate		**Minimal**		**Good**		**Excellent**

___ 1.1 There are not at least three examples of routine maintenance for the facility.[a]

___ 3.1 D There are at least three examples of routine maintenance for the facility.[a]

___ 5.1 D There are at least five examples of routine maintenance for the facility.[a]

___ 7.1 D There are at least seven examples of routine maintenance for the facility.[a]

___ 1.2 Space with adult-sized furniture is not provided for staff use during breaks, meetings, conferences, and preparation time (dual use of space is allowed).

___ 3.2 O Space with adult-sized furniture is provided for staff use during breaks, meetings, conferences, and preparation time (dual use of space is allowed).

___ 5.2 O Space is provided for meeting the individual needs of staff.[b]

___ 7.2 O There is dedicated space for staff use only that includes a professional library.[c]

Rationale:

Circle the final score based on the scoring rules on pages 5–6.

1   2   3   4   5   6   7

7. Facilities

8. Risk Management

a   A risk management plan can be a part of another document (e.g., operational handbook), but must be clearly labeled risk management plan.

b   The center's risk management plan **must** include:

- ❏ clear procedures to follow in the event of an emergency (e.g., chemical release/spill, fire, flood, intruder, pandemic, severe storm)

- ❏ clear procedures to reduce the risk of allegations of child abuse or neglect (e.g., an "open door" policy for families, consistent use of accident reports, daily sign-in and sign-out by families)

- ❏ clear procedures to maintain the safety of people, facilities, equipment, and/or materials (e.g., implementing universal precautions, sanitizing toys, servicing the fire extinguishers or alarm system, ensuring adequate ventilation in enclosed spaces, utilization of personal protective equipment, participating in a community-wide emergency preparedness plan)

c   Credit can be received when information on children's allergies and chronic medical conditions is posted in a confidential manner.

d   A system to ensure that emergency medical information is available to all teaching staff and substitutes **must** include:

- ❏ tangible, concrete evidence _____

- ❏ involvement of multiple individuals _____

- ❏ a defined process of accountability _____

e   To receive credit for this indicator, the form used to record drills must provide a designated space for areas in need of improvement and there must be at least two improvements noted during the past 12 months.

f   A system to ensure that emergency drills occur as planned **must** include:

- ❏ tangible, concrete evidence _____

- ❏ involvement of multiple individuals _____

- ❏ a defined process of accountability _____

g   CPR training must be specific for all age groups served (infant: birth to 12 months; child: one to eight years; school-age child/adult: eight years and older).

8. Risk Management

	1	2	3	4	5	6	7
	Inadequate		Minimal		Good		Excellent

___ 1.1 No risk management plan is available.[a]

___ 3.1 D A risk management plan is available.[a,b]

___ 5.1 O A risk management plan is available in each classroom.[a,b]

___ 7.1 D The risk management plan is reviewed annually.[a,b]

___ 1.2 Information on individual children's allergies is not posted in the classroom **and** information about children's chronic medical conditions is not kept in the office files.[c]

___ 3.2 O Information on individual children's allergies is posted in the classroom **and** information about children's chronic medical conditions is kept in the office files.[c]

___ 5.2 O Information about individual children's chronic medical conditions is kept in the children's classrooms as well as in the office files.[c]

___ 7.2 D A system is in place to ensure that all teaching staff (including substitute teachers) are made aware of necessary medical information.[c,d]

___ 1.3 During the past year, fire drills were not practiced once a month.

___ 3.3 D During the past year, fire drills were practiced once a month **and** indoor emergency drills (e.g., severe storms, intruder) were practiced twice a year.

___ 5.3 D The fire and indoor emergency drill records include improvements needed.[e]

___ 7.3 D A system is in place to ensure that fire drills and indoor emergency drills occur as planned.[f]

___ 1.4 The center does not have at least one staff person certified in CPR and First Aid assigned in each classroom.[g]

___ 3.4 D The center has at least one staff person certified in CPR and First Aid assigned in each classroom.[g]

___ 5.4 D The center provides CPR and First Aid training for staff at no cost at least every two years.[g]

___ 7.4 D All teaching staff are certified in CPR and First Aid.[g]

Rationale:

Circle the final score based on the scoring rules on pages 5–6.

1   2   3   4   5   6   7

8. Risk Management

9. Marketing and Public Relations

Notes

a   Public relations tools **may** include:

☐ advertising copy

☐ brochure

☐ business cards

☐ e-mail signature with contact information

☐ letterhead

☐ logo

☐ newsletter/eblast

☐ promotional item (e.g., clothing, mugs, caps)

☐ signage

☐ social media posts

☐ social networking page

☐ website

☐ other _____

b   *Project a professional image* refers to when the center uses a consistent logo on all promotional materials and the promotional materials are neat and grammatically correct. A proper noun (e.g., Kids' Kampus) is an exception to this rule.

c   *Key constituents* refers to at least one person from at least two groups (e.g., families, center staff, governing/advisory board, affiliated organization with oversight of the center). Key constituents do not need to be on-site.

9. Marketing and Public Relations

	1	2	3	4	5	6	7
	Inadequate		**Minimal**		**Good**		**Excellent**

___ 1.1 The center utilizes fewer than three public relations tools.[a]

___ 3.1 D The center utilizes five or more public relations tools.[a]

___ 5.1 D The center utilizes seven or more public relations tools.[a]

___ 7.1 D The center has a written policy that provides an incentive (e.g., cash/gift card, tuition discount) to families for referrals for new enrollment.

___ 1.2 Public relations tools do not project a professional image.[b]

___ 3.2 D Public relations tools project a professional image.[b]

___ 5.2 D Public relations tools are reviewed to ensure content is updated **and** images are inclusive (e.g., diverse race, ethnicity, ability, gender, family structure).

___ 7.2 D There was a review by key constituents of the public relations tools within the last three years.[c]

___ 1.3 Information about the center is not sent out, nor are follow-up calls made in response to inquiries within one business day.

___ 3.3 Information about the center is sent out and/or follow-up calls are made in response to inquiries within one business day.

___ 5.3 D Records are kept of all prospective families who inquire about the center **and** the follow-up action taken (e.g., call made, letter sent).

___ 7.3 D The center has a guide to train staff in providing information to prospective families who call or visit.

Rationale:

Circle the final score based on the scoring rules on pages 5–6.

1   2   3   4   5   6   7

9. Marketing and Public Relations

10. Technology

a   Examples of use of technology for recordkeeping **may** include:

- ❒ annual operating budget (projected revenue and expenditures)
- ❒ cash-flow projections
- ❒ donor database
- ❒ employee benefits (e.g., record of paid time off)
- ❒ enrollment database
- ❒ family database
- ❒ income and expenses statement (e.g., actuals)
- ❒ payroll record
- ❒ other _____

b   Examples of information security practices **may** include:

- ❒ backing up documents (saving documents in more than one medium)
- ❒ backing up internal hard drive
- ❒ encrypting/protecting sensitive data (e.g., social security numbers, credit card numbers)
- ❒ ensuring computers have firewall protection activated
- ❒ interacting with secure websites only
- ❒ limiting authority to install software on center devices
- ❒ limiting staff access to sensitive data or information
- ❒ removing former employees from electronic data access on their last day of employment
- ❒ requiring dual (two-factor) authentication for access to online accounts
- ❒ requiring staff to change passwords for computer access at least four times a year
- ❒ requiring staff to have individual log-ins and passwords for shared devices
- ❒ requiring staff to lock/password protect center devices while not in use (e.g., computer, tablet, cellular phone)
- ❒ restricting pop-ups on center computers
- ❒ storing sensitive data in a secure location (e.g., password protected electronic files)
- ❒ training staff on information security practices at least annually
- ❒ updating security software
- ❒ using a confidentiality form to protect against third-party risk (e.g., web designer access, payroll service)
- ❒ using only secure Internet networks
- ❒ other _____

c   A *comprehensive policy* regarding staff use of technology **must** include specific guidelines for staff regarding:

- ❒ digital confidentiality of work-related information
- ❒ e-mail etiquette
- ❒ personal use of the center's technology resources
- ❒ use of media releases (e.g., permission to use image, voice, and/or name in various media projects)
- ❒ use of social media

10. Technology

	1	2		3	4		5	6		7
	Inadequate			**Minimal**			**Good**			**Excellent**

___ 1.1 Administrative staff do not use technology for recordkeeping.[a]

___ 1.2 The center does not have at least two information security practices in place.[b]

___ 1.3 There is no policy regarding staff use of technology.

___ 3.1 D Administrative staff use technology for recordkeeping in three or more ways.[a]

___ 3.2 D The center has at least two information security practices in place.[b]

___ 3.3 D There is a policy regarding staff use of technology.

___ 5.1 D Administrative staff use technology for recordkeeping in six or more ways.[a]

___ 5.2 D The center has at least four information security practices in place.[b]

___ 5.3 D The policy regarding staff use of technology includes the acceptable or unacceptable use of computer, e-mail, and cell phone or other mobile device.

___ 7.1 D Job-specific technology training was provided for administrative staff within the past year.

___ 7.2 D The center has at least six information security practices in place.[b]

___ 7.3 D There is a comprehensive policy regarding staff use of technology.[c]

Rationale:

Circle the final score based on the scoring rules on pages 5–6.

1   2   3   4   5   6   7

10. Technology

Screening and Assessment

11. Screening and Identification (N/A is Allowed)

Notes

Item 11 may be scored N/A for a program serving *only* school-age children.

a *Screening* refers to the first step in a two-step process to identify children with potential disabilities and/or challenges in learning or development. A screening tool is administered to determine if a referral for further evaluation is necessary. A screening tool is used to screen children across multiple developmental domains.

b *Are screened* refers to making developmental screening available to all children birth to five.

c *Valid and reliable screening tools* refers to published research-based tools (e.g., Ages and Stages, Brigance, Early Screening Inventory).

d Safeguards (for each screening tool utilized) **must** include:

❒ screening is administered by a qualified individual(s)

❒ screening is interpreted by a qualified professional(s)

❒ multiple sources of evidence are used (e.g., family and staff input based on home and center observations)

❒ children are screened in their primary language

e Specialists **may** include:

❒ Behavior Specialist

❒ Developmental Therapist

❒ Early Intervention Specialist

❒ Mental Health Consultant

❒ Physical Therapist (PT)

❒ Occupational Therapist (OT)

❒ Social Worker

❒ Speech and Language Pathologist (SLP)

❒ other _____

f Collaboration, at a minimum, requires two-way communication between a staff member(s) and a specialist(s). To meet the requirements of this indicator, the system must support communication that is initiated from staff-to-specialists and from specialists-to-staff.

The required elements of a system to support collaboration with specialists are met if there is an Individualized Education Plan (IEP) or an Individualized Family Service Plan (IFSP) that includes the Administrator and/or a staff member from the center.

A system to support collaboration with specialists **must** include:

❒ tangible, concrete evidence _____

❒ involvement of multiple individuals _____

❒ a defined process of accountability _____

Screening and Assessment

11. Screening and Identification (N/A is allowed)

1	2	3	4	5	6	7
Inadequate		Minimal		Good		Excellent

___ 1.1 Children are not screened.[a]

___ 3.1 D All children, birth to 5 years of age, are screened.[a,b]

___ 5.1 D All children, birth to 5 years of age, are screened using a valid and reliable screening tool.[a,b,c]

___ 7.1 D To protect against misidentification, safeguards are built into the screening process.[a,d]

___ 1.2 Consent is not obtained from the family prior to screening (N/A is allowed when another organization conducts the screening and is responsible for obtaining consent).[a]

___ 3.2 D Consent is obtained from the family as a prerequisite to screening (N/A is allowed when another organization conducts the screening and is responsible for obtaining consent).[a]

___ 5.2 D All families are informed of the results of screening regardless of the findings.[a]

___ 7.2 D Families are informed if further evaluation is recommended and a referral with contact information is provided.

___ 1.3 Space and time are not available on-site for a specialist to work with children with identified needs.[e]

___ 3.3 Space and time are available on-site for a specialist to work with children with identified needs.[e]

___ 5.3 D A specialist works with children with identified needs in their classroom.[e]

___ 7.3 D A system is in place to support collaboration with specialists working with children with identified needs.[e,f]

Rationale:

Circle the final score based on the scoring rules on pages 5–6.

1   2   3   4   5   6   7   N/A

11. Screening and Identification

12. Assessment in Support of Learning (N/A is allowed)

Notes

Assessment in support of learning provides data to support teaching staff in improving their practice and children's learning outcomes.

Item 12 may be scored N/A for a program serving *only* school-age children.

a *Valid and reliable assessment* refers to a published research-based tool (e.g., High/Scope COR, Work Sampling System, Teaching Strategies GOLD).

b Multiple measures to assess children's learning and development **may** include:

❑ audio recordings

❑ contextualized photos

❑ observation notes

❑ portfolio sampling of children's work

❑ video recordings

❑ other _____

c *Curriculum* refers to a framework that guides the intentional implementation of activities in support of children's learning and development.

d *Standards* refer to national or state recognized early learning and development guidelines.

e *Aggregated assessment results* refers to when individual children's assessments are combined for the purpose of analysis. The purpose of aggregating is to look for trends to inform program improvement efforts.

Disaggregated assessment results refers to when data are broken down into components (e.g., ethnicity, gender, geographic region, language, race). The purpose of disaggregated assessment results is to identify any inequitable child outcomes, evaluate practices, and plan for improvements.

12. Assessment in Support of Learning (N/A is allowed)

1	2	3	4	5	6	7
Inadequate		**Minimal**		**Good**		**Excellent**

___ 1.1 Teaching staff do not use an assessment tool to assess children's learning and development.

___ 3.1 D Teaching staff use an assessment tool to assess children's learning and development.

___ 5.1 D Teaching staff use a valid and reliable assessment tool to assess children in each age group served, birth to 5 years of age.[a]

___ 7.1 D In addition to using a valid and reliable assessment tool, teaching staff use multiple measures to assess children's learning and development.[a,b]

___ 1.2 The center does not use an identified curriculum.[c]

___ 3.2 D The center uses an identified curriculum aligned with learning and development standards.[c,d]

___ 5.2 D Lesson plans indicate the specific learning and development standards addressed.[d]

___ 7.2 D Lesson plans indicate the specific learning and development standards addressed and are shared with families (e.g., bulletin board, newsletter, website).[d]

___ 1.3 Individual child assessment results are not utilized by teaching staff in lesson planning.

___ 3.3 D Individual child assessment results are utilized by teaching staff in lesson planning.

___ 5.3 D Teaching staff working with the same group of children implement plan-do-study-act cycles to continuously improve teaching practices.

___ 7.3 D Aggregated **and** disaggregated child assessment results are utilized by administrative staff in long-range planning and/or program evaluation.[e]

Rationale:

Circle the final score based on the scoring rules on pages 5–6.

| 1 | 2 | 3 | 4 | 5 | 6 | 7 | N/A |

12. Assessment in Support of Learning

Fiscal Management

13. Budget Planning

a A *needs assessment* refers to an inquiry process in which center staff identify any gaps between what currently exists (e.g., supplies, equipment, staff, and other resources) and what is needed (e.g., supplies, equipment, staff, and other resources) to improve or enhance early care and education services. Needs are prioritized for budget planning.

b Revenues **may** include:

- ❑ Child and Adult Care Food Program
- ❑ Child Care Assistance Program (e.g., subsidy voucher)
- ❑ contract
- ❑ fundraising
- ❑ grant (public or private)
- ❑ gift
- ❑ tuition/fee
- ❑ other _____

Expenditures **may** include:

- ❑ accreditation
- ❑ benefits
- ❑ deferred equipment replacement/capital improvements
- ❑ food
- ❑ insurance
- ❑ maintenance
- ❑ marketing
- ❑ professional development
- ❑ professional services (e.g., accounting, legal, shared services)
- ❑ rent/mortgage

- ❑ salaries
- ❑ supplies
- ❑ transportation
- ❑ utilities
- ❑ other _____

c Use the following grid to determine when the fourth quarter begins:

Fiscal year begins	Fourth quarter begins
January 1	October 1
July 1	April 1
October 1	July 1

d Accepted practices that provide for adequate cash flow **may** include:

- ❑ clear policy/procedure regarding the collection of delinquent tuition/fees
- ❑ clear policy/procedure to maintain adequate attendance levels
- ❑ collection of tuition/fees handled by a third party (e.g., shared services alliance)
- ❑ method for informing parents about money owed
- ❑ prompt deposit of income
- ❑ other _____

e Quarterly cash-flow projections are developed from the operating budget and provide a summary of anticipated revenue and expenditures at three-month intervals.

Fiscal Management

13. Budget Planning

1	2	3	4	5	6	7
Inadequate		Minimal		Good		Excellent

___ 1.1 The Administrator does not develop, inform, or review the center's operating budget before it is finalized.

___ 3.1 The Administrator develops, informs, or reviews the center's operating budget before it is finalized.

___ 5.1 There is a needs assessment
D conducted prior to finalizing the operating budget.[a]

___ 7.1 The operating budget reflects
D the priorities identified from the needs assessment.[a]

___ 1.2 There is no current year operating budget.

___ 3.2 The current year operating
D budget includes revenue and expenditures with line-item breakdowns.[b]

___ 5.2 The current operating budget has
D a minimum of three line-item breakdowns for revenues and nine for expenditures.[b]

___ 7.2 A draft operating budget for
D the next fiscal year is available by the beginning of the fourth quarter of the **current** fiscal year.[c]

___ 1.3 Payroll, insurance, and taxes are not always paid on time.

___ 3.3 Payroll, insurance, and taxes are always paid on time.

___ 5.3 There are at least two accepted
D practices to provide for adequate cash flow.[d]

___ 7.3 Quarterly cash-flow projections
D are available.[e]

Rationale:

Circle the final score based on the scoring rules on pages 5–6.

1   2   3   4   5   6   7

13. Budget Planning

14. Accounting Practices

Notes

a Credit is given if income and expense statements are generated quarterly or more frequently (i.e., monthly).

b Checks and balances **may** include:

- ❏ receipts required for petty cash used
- ❏ separation of duties (e.g., the same person does not receive cash and authorize cash disbursements)
- ❏ separation of restricted funds (e.g., grants, endowment, and major capital funds) from general operating funds
- ❏ sign-in and sign-out required for use of business credit card
- ❏ two or more people approve expenditures
- ❏ two or more signatures required on checks
- ❏ two or more signatures required on purchase orders
- ❏ other _____

c *Independent third party* means that the reviewer is not an employee of the early childhood center. A board member, family member, or administrator of an affiliated agency with oversight of the center can conduct an independent review.

d Credit is given if the review happens quarterly or more frequently (i.e., monthly).

14. Accounting Practices

	1	2		3	4		5	6		7
	Inadequate			**Minimal**			**Good**			**Excellent**

___ 1.1 An income and expense statement is not generated quarterly.[a]

___ 3.1 D An income and expense statement is generated quarterly.[a]

___ 5.1 D The Administrator has access to or generates quarterly income and expense statements.[a]

___ 7.1 D The Administrator compares quarterly income and expense statements to quarterly cash-flow projections to monitor the center's fiscal status.

___ 1.2 There is not at least one example of accounting checks and balances.[b]

___ 3.2 D There is at least one example of accounting checks and balances.[b]

___ 5.2 D There are at least two examples of accounting checks and balances.[b]

___ 7.2 D There are at least three examples of accounting checks and balances.[b]

___ 1.3 There is no monthly review of the accounting records (e.g., reconciliation of bank and/or credit card statements, comparison of income and expenses).

___ 3.3 D There is a monthly review of the accounting records (e.g., reconciliation of bank and/or credit card statements, comparison of income and expenses).

___ 5.3 D There is a quarterly review of the accounting records by an independent third party.[c,d]

___ 7.3 D An outside audit is conducted annually by a certified public accountant.

Rationale:

Circle the final score based on the scoring rules on pages 5–6.

1   2   3   4   5   6   7

14. Accounting Practices

Organizational Growth and Development

15. Strategic Planning

Notes

Evidence of strategic planning (a mission or vision statement and a strategic plan) must specifically address the early care and education program.

a A *mission* is a succinct statement of the center's purpose for existence that informs strategic decision-making. A *vision* is a statement of an ideal that can be used to motivate, inspire, and guide the center toward a desired future state.

b A strategic plan differs from an annual program improvement plan because the scope of work requires more than one year to achieve goals.

c A comprehensive strategic plan is a document that **must** include:
- ❐ needs assessment (gap analysis of the early care and education needs of families, staff, and/or community)
- ❐ timeframe
- ❐ strategic priorities (long-term goals)
- ❐ objectives
- ❐ strategies to achieve goals (e.g., marketing, construction, enrollment, staffing, compensation, or financial plans)

15. Strategic Planning

1	2	3	4	5	6	7
Inadequate		Minimal		Good		Excellent

___ 1.1 The center does not have a mission or vision statement.[a]

___ 1.2 The center's mission or vison statement is not included in the family handbook.[a]

___ 1.3 The center does not have a strategic plan.[b]

___ 3.1 D The center has a mission or vision statement.[a]

___ 3.2 D The center's mission or vision statement is included in the family handbook.[a]

___ 3.3 D The center has a strategic plan.[b]

___ 5.1 D Staff and families are involved in developing or reviewing the center's mission or vision statement.[a]

___ 5.2 D The center's mission or vision statement is included in the family **and** staff handbooks.[a]

___ 5.3 D The center has a comprehensive strategic plan.[b,c]

___ 7.1 D Staff, families, and at least one external representative (e.g., affiliated agency, business, public school, subject matter expert) are involved in developing and/or reviewing the center's mission or vision statement.[a]

___ 7.2 O The center's mission or vision statement is displayed in classrooms.[a]

___ 7.3 D Staff, families, and at least one external representative (e.g., affiliated agency, business, public school, subject matter expert) are involved in developing the center's comprehensive strategic plan.[b,c]

Rationale:

Circle the final score based on the scoring rules on pages 5–6.

1   2   3   4   5   6   7

15. Strategic Planning

16. Evaluation and Continuous Improvement

Notes

a   Examples of published observation tools to measure teaching and learning **may** include the following:

- ❐ Classroom Assessment and Scoring System (CLASS)
- ❐ Environment Rating Scales (ERS)
- ❐ Classroom Observation Tool, National Association for the Education of Young Children (NAEYC)
- ❐ other _____

b   Examples of ways to obtain feedback from staff about the quality of the overall program **may** include:

- ❐ agenda item at staff meeting
- ❐ published assessment tool
- ❐ exit interview
- ❐ informal questionnaire
- ❐ message book
- ❐ suggestion box
- ❐ other _____

c   Examples of published assessment tools for staff to evaluate overall program quality **may** include:

- ❐ Early Childhood Work Environment Survey (ECWES)
- ❐ Essential 0–5 Survey
- ❐ Program Observation Tool, National Association for the Education of Young Children (NAEYC)
- ❐ Supportive Environmental Quality Underlying Adult Learning (SEQUAL) Survey
- ❐ other _____

d   Examples of ways to obtain feedback from families **may** include:

- ❐ agenda item at family meeting
- ❐ published assessment tool
- ❐ exit interview
- ❐ individual family conference
- ❐ informal questionnaire
- ❐ message book
- ❐ suggestion box
- ❐ other _____

e   Examples of published assessment tools for families to evaluate overall program quality **may** include:

- ❐ Head Start Family Survey
- ❐ Parent Satisfaction Survey
- ❐ other _____

16. Evaluation and Continuous Improvement

1	2	3	4	5	6	7
Inadequate		**Minimal**		**Good**		**Excellent**

____ 1.1 The center does not use an observation tool to measure teaching and learning.[a]

____ 3.1 D The center uses an observation tool to measure teaching and learning.[a]

____ 5.1 D Teaching staff meet at least quarterly to participate in plan-do-study-act cycles to improve teaching and learning.

____ 7.1 D Teaching staff meet at least once per month to participate in plan-do-study-act cycles to improve teaching and learning.

____ 1.2 The center does not obtain feedback from staff about the quality of the overall program in at least one way.[b]

____ 3.2 D The center obtains feedback from staff about the quality of the overall program in three or more ways.[b]

____ 5.2 D An assessment tool was used by staff to evaluate the quality of the overall program at least once in the last three years.[c]

____ 7.2 D An assessment tool is used annually by staff to evaluate the quality of the overall program.[c]

____ 1.3 The center does not obtain feedback from families about the quality of the overall program in at least one way.[d]

____ 3.3 D The center obtains feedback from families about the quality of the overall program in three or more ways.[d]

____ 5.3 D An assessment tool was used by families to evaluate the quality of the overall program at least once in the last three years.[e]

____ 7.3 D An assessment tool is used annually by families to evaluate the quality of the overall program.[e]

____ 1.4 Program decision-making is not influenced by staff **or** family feedback about the quality of the overall program.

____ 3.4 Program decision-making is influenced by staff **and** family feedback about the quality of the overall program.

____ 5.4 D The center's evaluation process includes a feedback loop to staff **and** families.

____ 7.4 D Data from staff **and** family evaluations are used to develop a written plan for program improvement.

Rationale:

Circle the final score based on the scoring rules on pages 5–6.

1   2   3   4   5   6   7

16. Evaluation and Continuous Improvement

Family and Community Partnerships

17. Family Communications

Notes

a   Written information **must** include:
- ❏ children's daily schedule
- ❏ discipline and guidance policy
- ❏ family supports
- ❏ health requirements
- ❏ hours of operation
- ❏ notification of days the center is closed (e.g., holidays, professional development)
- ❏ program mission or vision statement
- ❏ tuition/fee policy (N/A is allowed for centers at which no tuition or fees are charged)

b   Orientation practices **may** include:
- ❏ calling new family to check in
- ❏ convening an orientation meeting for new families
- ❏ determining family's preferred language for verbal and written communication
- ❏ discussing identified disability/need and plan for reasonable accommodation
- ❏ introducing new family to the teaching and administrative staff
- ❏ pairing new family with a mentor family
- ❏ providing home visit
- ❏ providing informal opportunity to ask questions of the Administrator
- ❏ sharing information regarding community services and/or supports
- ❏ other _____

c   *Enrollment* refers to the first step in the orientation process.

d   A system to check in with new families **must** include:
- ❏ tangible, concrete evidence _____
- ❏ involvement of multiple individuals _____
- ❏ a defined process of accountability _____

e   Modes of communication **may** include:
- ❏ adaptive measure (e.g., sign language, telecommunication device for the deaf, translation)
- ❏ bulletin board
- ❏ communication app (e.g., Brightwheel, GroupMe, ProCare)
- ❏ e-mail
- ❏ family meeting
- ❏ individual conference
- ❏ informal in-person conversation
- ❏ mailed letter
- ❏ message book
- ❏ newsletter
- ❏ note that goes home with children
- ❏ phone call/voicemail
- ❏ social media group for enrolled families
- ❏ text messaging
- ❏ two-way communication log between teachers and families
- ❏ video conferencing (e.g. Microsoft Teams, Webex, Zoom)
- ❏ website
- ❏ other _____

f   Two-way communication may be initiated by teaching staff-to-families or by families-to-teaching staff. A system to support daily two-way communication between teaching staff and families **must** include:
- ❏ tangible, concrete evidence _____
- ❏ involvement of multiple individuals _____
- ❏ a defined process of accountability _____

Family and Community Partnerships

17. Family Communications

	1	2	3	4	5	6	7
	Inadequate		**Minimal**		**Good**		**Excellent**

___ 1.1 The center does not share written information with new families during orientation.

___ 3.1 D The center shares written information with new families during orientation.[a]

___ 5.1 D The center implements at least three family orientation practices designed to build trusting relationships between staff and families.[b]

___ 7.1 D The center has a system to check in with new families within 45 days of enrollment.[c,d]

___ 1.2 Information about child, family, and community (e.g., child's strengths and likes, culture, extended family, daily routines, childrearing practices, neighborhood supports) is not solicited during enrollment.[c]

___ 3.2 D Information about child, family, and community (e.g., child's strengths and likes, culture, extended family, daily routines, childrearing practices, neighborhood supports) is solicited during enrollment.[c]

___ 5.2 D Information about child, family, and community (e.g., child's strengths and likes, culture, extended family, daily routines, childrearing practices, neighborhood supports) is solicited during conferences.

___ 7.2 D Based on information shared during enrollment and/or conferences, staff adjust practices to achieve consistency between home and center when possible.[c]

___ 1.3 The center does not communicate with families in their preferred language or utilize resources as needed to communicate with families.

___ 3.3 The center communicates with families in their preferred language or utilizes resources as needed to communicate with families.

___ 5.3 D The center communicates with families by using eight or more modes of communication.[e]

___ 7.3 D The center communicates with families by using twelve or more modes of communication.[e]

___ 1.4 The center does not provide formal conferencing to discuss children's learning and development. (N/A allowed if center serves **only** school age children.)

___ 3.4 D The center provides one formal conference per year to discuss children's learning and development at times that are convenient for working families. (N/A allowed if center serves **only** school age children.)

___ 5.4 D The center provides two formal conferences per year to discuss children's learning and development at times that are convenient for working families. (N/A allowed if center serves **only** school age children.)

___ 7.4 D A system exists to support daily two-way communication between teaching staff and families.[f] (N/A allowed if center serves **only** school age children.)

Rationale:

Circle the final score based on the scoring rules on pages 5–6.

1	2	3	4	5	6	7

17. Family Communications

18. Family Support and Engagment

Notes

a *Family supports* refers to the variety of ways that a center can be responsive to family needs. Examples of family supports **may** include:

- ❏ adult class (e.g., computer, ESL, GED, employment support)
- ❏ child care during family conferences or meetings taking place outside of program hours
- ❏ children's book or toy lending library
- ❏ convenience service (e.g., take-home meals, photographs)
- ❏ discount coupon for community events or services
- ❏ extended care during evenings or weekends
- ❏ family meeting, seminar, or support group
- ❏ family resource library
- ❏ family-to-family mentorship opportunity
- ❏ food, clothing, or supply donation
- ❏ information and/or referral to supportive service
- ❏ home visit
- ❏ social function for families and staff
- ❏ transition planning to kindergarten/new program
- ❏ transportation to and from the center
- ❏ tuition scholarship
- ❏ other _____

b *A governing/advisory board* refers to a group of three or more people (e.g., staff member, family member, business representative, school district representative, subject matter expert) who provide the center with the benefit of multiple perspectives to guide strategic direction and determine program priorities. The *governing board* has **additional** responsibilities for fiscal oversight and governance (required if the center is organized as a nonprofit organization).

c The communication must describe the activity **and** how it promotes children's learning and development.

d *At-home learning activities* **may** include:

- ❏ reading and discussing selected books related to classroom themes
- ❏ games for families to do together that expand on learning concepts
- ❏ puzzles for families to do together to enhance spatial recognition
- ❏ other _____

18. Family Support and Engagement

	1	2	3	4	5	6	7
	Inadequate		**Minimal**		**Good**		**Excellent**

___ 1.1 The center offers no family supports.[a]

___ 3.1 D The center offers at least four family supports.[a]

___ 5.1 D The center offers at least eight family supports.[a]

___ 7.1 D The center offers at least twelve family supports.[a]

___ 1.2 There is no plan for involving families in the activities of the center.

___ 3.2 D Families participate in educational meetings, special events, parties, and/or field trips.

___ 5.2 D Families engage in daily classroom routines (e.g., free play, reading books, story dictation, cooking projects).

___ 7.2 D A minimum of one family member serves on the center's governing/advisory board.[b]

___ 1.3 The expertise of families regarding their children's strengths and needs is not valued.

___ 3.3 The expertise of families regarding their children's strengths and needs is valued.

___ 5.3 D Teaching staff communicate with families in multiple ways about the learning activities occurring in the classroom (e.g., conversation, displayed narrative accompanying photos or work sample, letter, memo, newsletter).[c]

___ 7.3 D Families engage in at-home learning activities made available for the purpose of extending the classroom learning.[d]

Rationale:

Circle the final score based on the scoring rules on pages 5–6.

1   2   3   4   5   6   7

18. Family Support and Engagement

19. Community Outreach

Notes

a *Early childhood professional community* refers to a national, state, regional, or local organization, network, or collaboration with a primary focus on early childhood education and care.

b *Involvement* means that the Administrator and/or a center staff member participate in an early childhood focused network/collaboration, are members of a national, state, regional, or local early childhood organization, or collaborate with the local elementary school.

c *Active role* means the Administrator and/or center staff member attend at least half of regularly scheduled meetings.

d *Leadership role* means that the Administrator and/or center staff member chair a committee, serve on an advisory council or board, or hold office.

e *Community organization* refers to a local business, civic, or faith-based organization that is **not** primarily concerned with early childhood education and care.

Examples of community organizations **may** include:

- ❑ business roundtable
- ❑ chamber of commerce
- ❑ church, synagogue, mosque, or temple
- ❑ city or town council
- ❑ college/university
- ❑ community development agency
- ❑ food pantry
- ❑ League of Women Voters

- ❑ Neighborhood Watch Program
- ❑ Rotary International
- ❑ United Way
- ❑ YWCA, YMCA
- ❑ other _____

19. Community Outreach

	1	2		3	4		5	6		7
	Inadequate			**Minimal**			**Good**			**Excellent**

___ 1.1 The Administrator or center staff member have no involvement in the early childhood professional community.[a,b]

___ 3.1 D The Administrator and/or center staff member have some involvement in the early childhood professional community.[a,b]

___ 5.1 D The Administrator and/or center staff member play an active role in the early childhood professional community.[a,c]

___ 7.1 D The Administrator and/or center staff member played a leadership role in the early childhood professional community during the past three years.[a,d]

___ 1.2 The Administrator or center staff member do not attend two or more events per year in the community.

___ 3.2 D The Administrator and/or center staff member attend two or more events per year in the community.

___ 5.2 D The Administrator and/or center staff member play an active role in at least one community organization.[c,e]

___ 7.2 D The Administrator and/or center staff member have played a leadership role in at least one community organization during the past three years.[d,e]

___ 1.3 The center does not demonstrate concern for being a good neighbor. (e.g., posts reminders about parking restrictions, participates in a neighborhood watch program, hosts food or clothing drive).

___ 3.3 D The center demonstrates concern for being a good neighbor (e.g., posts reminders about parking restrictions, participates in a neighborhood watch program, hosts food or clothing drive).

___ 5.3 D The center demonstrates efforts to build good relations with the community (e.g., provides intergenerational program, collaborates in transition planning with other organizations, participates in events such as working a booth at a fair or marching in a neighborhood parade).

___ 7.3 D There is evidence of support from the community (e.g., financial, in-kind donated services, tangible gifts, discounted services, letters of recommendation).

Rationale:

Circle the final score based on the scoring rules on pages 5–6.

1   2   3   4   5   6   7

19. Community Outreach

Relational Leadership

20. Meetings and Shared Decision-Making

Notes

a *Centerwide staff meetings* refers to meetings that occur at a time when all staff are together. Meetings may involve a training component, but training is not the main purpose of the meeting.

b Participation in planning for centerwide staff meetings **may** include:

❐ identifying any resource needed for the meeting

❐ identifying facilitator for each agenda item

❐ identifying the length of time needed for agenda items

❐ identifying the priority level of agenda items

❐ identifying whether a decision is needed for agenda items

❐ other _____

c *Minutes* refers to a written record of topics discussed and what occurred at the meeting.

d An action plan **must** identify at least **three** of the following:

❐ specific activities to be completed

❐ person responsible

❐ resources needed

❐ timeline

❐ evaluation checkpoints

e *Agenda* refers to a written record of what topics will be addressed at a staff meeting.

f *Collaborative decision-making* refers to when staff define and analyze problems together and decide on a course of action. The final decision is made by unanimous vote, majority vote, or consensus vote.

g *Delegated decision-making* refers to when a decision is entrusted to a subgroup of the staff or an individual staff member.

Relational Leadership

20. Meetings and Shared Decision-Making

	1	2	3	4	5	6	7
	Inadequate		**Minimal**		**Good**		**Excellent**

___ 1.1 There are not at least two scheduled, centerwide staff meetings per year.[a]	___ 3.1 D	There are at least two scheduled, centerwide staff meetings per year.[a]	___ 5.1 D	There are scheduled staff meetings that occur at least once a month (may include team or centerwide meetings).[a]	___ 7.1 D There are scheduled staff meetings that occur at least twice a month (may include team or centerwide meetings).[a]
___ 1.2 Staff do not contribute agenda items to be included in centerwide staff meetings.[a]	___ 3.2 D	Staff contribute agenda items to be included in centerwide staff meetings.[a]	___ 5.2 D	Teaching staff participate in planning for centerwide staff meetings.[a,b]	___ 7.2 D Teaching staff facilitate the discussion of agenda items during the majority of centerwide staff meetings.[a]
___ 1.3 Minutes are not generated from staff meetings.[c]	___ 3.3 D	Minutes are generated from staff meetings.[c]	___ 5.3 D	Minutes for staff meetings reflect an action plan.[c,d]	___ 7.3 D Minutes are distributed in advance of staff meetings **and** action plans are revisited at subsequent meetings.[c,d]
___ 1.4 Staff meetings do not have an agenda that is distributed (paper or electronic) to participants.[e]	___ 3.4 D	Staff meetings have an agenda that is distributed (paper or electronic) to participants.[e]	___ 5.4 D	Staff meetings have an agenda that includes a facilitator for each agenda item, time limits for each agenda item, **and** an identified notetaker.[e]	___ 7.4 D There are guidelines for staff meetings (e.g., seek first to understand then speak, everyone has the right to pass, limit side conversations, respect differences of opinion, silence cell phones).
___ 1.5 Minutes from staff meetings do not reflect decisions made.[c]	___ 3.5 D	Minutes from staff meetings reflect decisions made.[c]	___ 5.5 D	Minutes from staff meetings reflect either collaborative **or** delegated decision-making.[c,f,g]	___ 7.5 D Minutes from staff meetings reflect collaborative **and** delegated decision-making.[c,f,g]

Rationale:

Circle the final score based on the scoring rules on pages 5–6.

1   2   3   4   5   6   7

20. Meetings and Shared Decision-Making

21. Internal Communications

Notes

a   Examples of ways to communicate with staff **may** include:

- ☐ adaptive measure (e.g., sign language, telecommunication device for the deaf, translation)
- ☐ bulletin board
- ☐ communication app (e.g., GroupMe, WhatsApp)
- ☐ e-mail
- ☐ individual meeting
- ☐ informal conversation
- ☐ internal memo
- ☐ internal newsletter
- ☐ mailed letter

- ☐ message book
- ☐ phone call/voicemail
- ☐ routing slip
- ☐ shared document creation (e.g., track changes)
- ☐ staff meeting
- ☐ text messaging
- ☐ video conferencing (e.g. Microsoft Teams, Webex, Zoom)
- ☐ video messaging
- ☐ other _____

b   Strength-based practices to support staff **may** include:

- ☐ allocating resource to empower staff to demonstrate strengths (e.g., providing classroom coverage so that a new teacher can learn from an experienced teacher by observing in her classroom)
- ☐ coaching that builds on an individual's strengths to increase competencies
- ☐ identifying individual's strengths and interests during orientation
- ☐ mentorship program (e.g., paid time for experienced staff member to mentor new staff member)

- ☐ opportunity to model strengths (e.g., present on strength at staff meeting, provide demonstration in the classroom)
- ☐ performance appraisal process connecting individual's strengths to their performance
- ☐ practice demonstrating appreciation for one another's strengths (e.g., gratitude board, mindfulness exercise)
- ☐ reflective supervision that builds on individual's strengths
- ☐ resource to learn about strength-based approach (e.g., article, book, assessment, professional development)
- ☐ team-building activity based on strengths at staff meeting
- ☐ other _____

c   *Personal biases* refers to beliefs based on one's own lived experience resulting in prejudice (prejudgment) either for or against a position, person, or group.

d   A conflict resolution policy is more than a statement describing who to go to with a grievance. The policy **must** address conflict resolution in the context of the work environment and identify an expectation that peers work together to resolve their disputes using open, professional communication before requesting supervisor support.

21. Internal Communications

1	2	3	4	5	6	7
Inadequate		**Minimal**		**Good**		**Excellent**

___ 1.1 Information is not communicated in four or more ways.[a]

___ 1.2 The Administrator is not knowledgeable about a strength-based approach to supporting staff.

___ 1.3 The Administrator does not reflect on personal biases.[c]

___ 1.4 The center does not have resources to assist with conflict resolution (e.g., articles, books, training, videos).

___ 3.1 Information is communicated in four or more ways.[a]
D

___ 3.2 The Administrator is knowledgeable about a strength-based approach to supporting staff.

___ 3.3 The Administrator reflects on personal biases.[c]

___ 3.4 The center has resources to assist with conflict resolution (e.g., articles, books, training, videos).
D

___ 5.1 Information is communicated in seven or more ways.[a]
D

___ 5.2 At least four strength-based practices are implemented.[b]
D

___ 5.3 The Administrator provides opportunities for staff to reflect on personal biases and discuss how biases influence behavior.[c]
D

___ 5.4 There is a conflict resolution policy regarding the handling of staff disputes.[d]
D

___ 7.1 Information is communicated in ten or more ways.[a]
D

___ 7.2 At least six strength-based practices are implemented.[b]
D

___ 7.3 Staff review their professional practices from a diversity, equity, and inclusion (DEI) perspective and implement changes.
D

___ 7.4 There are procedures to guide staff implementation of a conflict resolution policy (behavior and/or communication strategies to be used).[d]
D

Rationale:

Circle the final score based on the scoring rules on pages 5–6.

1   2   3   4   5   6   7

21. Internal Communications

Staff Qualifications

22. Administrator

Notes

Administrator refers to the individual who has primary responsibility for planning, implementing, and evaluating the early childhood program. The Administrator must be located on-site if the center has four or more classrooms or a total enrollment of 60 or more full-time equivalent (FTE) children. Role titles for the Administrator vary and may include director, manager, coordinator, or principal.

Depending on the scope of services provided and the size of the early childhood program, there may be several individuals who have administrative roles. The rating for this item is based only on the qualifications of the individual designated as the Administrator.

a *Coursework in administration* refers to content related to one or more of the three domains of Whole Leadership (Leadership Essentials, Administrative Leadership, Pedagogical Leadership) and **may** include:

Leadership Essentials

- ❏ adult learning theory
- ❏ change management
- ❏ collaboration and team-building
- ❏ cultural competence
- ❏ ethical conduct
- ❏ oral and written communication
- ❏ organizational climate
- ❏ personal and professional self-awareness
- ❏ relational leadership (e.g., creating a trusting and appreciative culture, embedding shared decision-making)
- ❏ systems thinking
- ❏ other _____

Administrative Leadership

- ❏ advocacy
- ❏ fiscal management
- ❏ human resources development
- ❏ legal issues
- ❏ marketing and public relations
- ❏ operations (e.g., systems for risk management, facilities, technology)
- ❏ strategic planning and program evaluation
- ❏ other _____

Pedagogical Leadership

- ❏ application of adult learning theory and research to practice
- ❏ application of child development theory and research to practice
- ❏ coaching and mentoring
- ❏ culturally responsive teaching and leading
- ❏ family engagement (e.g., fostering family leadership, promoting partnerships)
- ❏ reflective supervision
- ❏ use of child assessment data to improve teaching and learning (e.g., cycles of continuous quality improvement)
- ❏ other _____

b *Administrative experience* refers to the responsibility for early childhood or school-age program planning, implementation, and evaluation. It can include experience as an assistant director or coordinator of a program component. A *year of experience* is defined as a minimum of 1,200 hours (a six-hour workday for an academic year).

52

Staff Qualifications

22. Administrator

	1	2	3	4	5	6	7
	Inadequate		**Minimal**		**Good**		**Excellent**

___ 1.1 The Administrator has less than an associate degree **or** 60 sh of college credit.	___ 3.1 D The Administrator has an associate degree **or** 60 sh of college credit.	___ 5.1 D The Administrator has a baccalaureate degree.	___ 7.1 D The Administrator has a graduate **or** other advanced degree.
___ 1.2 The Administrator has less than 18 sh of college credit for ECE/CD coursework.	___ 3.2 D The Administrator has 21 or more sh of college credit for ECE/CD coursework.	___ 5.2 D The Administrator has 24 or more sh of college credit for ECE/CD coursework.	___ 7.2 D The Administrator has 30 or more sh of college credit for ECE/CD coursework.
___ 1.3 The Administrator has no college credit for coursework in administration.[a]	___ 3.3 D The Administrator has 9 or more sh of college credit for coursework in administration.[a]	___ 5.3 D The Administrator has 15 or more sh of college credit for coursework in administration.[a]	___ 7.3 D The Administrator has 21 or more sh of college credit for coursework in administration.[a]
___ 1.4 The Administrator has less than one year of administrative experience.[b]	___ 3.4 D The Administrator has one or more years of administrative experience.[b]	___ 5.4 D The Administrator has three or more years of administrative experience.[b]	___ 7.4 D The Administrator has five or more years of administrative experience.[b]

Rationale:

Circle the final score based on the scoring rules on pages 5–6.

1   2   3   4   5   6   7

22. Administrator

23. Lead Teacher

Notes

Depending on the staffing pattern of the program, there may be several individuals working with a group of children who are responsible for their daily care and education.

Lead Teacher refers to the individual with the highest professional qualifications (includes level of general education, specialized coursework, and experience) assigned to teach a group of children and who is responsible for daily lesson planning, parent conferences, child assessment, and curriculum planning. This individual may also supervise other members of the teaching team. In some settings, this person is called a head teacher, master teacher, or teacher.

a A *year of experience* is defined as a minimum of 1,200 hours (a six-hour workday for an academic year).

Data Collection Procedures

1. Make copies of the **Teaching Staff Qualifications Worksheet** on page 63 so there is a separate worksheet for each group/classroom of children. At the top of the worksheet write the program name and the name of the group/classroom.

2. In the designated space, write the initials of each member of the teaching staff regularly assigned to each group/classroom. This worksheet provides space for up to four members of the teaching staff for each group/classroom.

3. Provide the information regarding general education, specialized education/training, experience, and credential/license of each member of the teaching staff regularly assigned to each group/classroom.

4. Determine which member of the teaching staff for each group/classroom will be designated as the Lead Teacher for purposes of completing Item 23 and designate all teaching roles for that classroom: Lead Teacher (LT), Teacher (T), or Assistant Teacher/Aide (ATA). Remember, there can only be one individual designated as the Lead Teacher in each classroom/group of children.

5. Make additional copies of Item 23 on page 55 so that each individual designated as Lead Teacher (one for each group/classroom of children) has a separate Item 23 page. Complete the rating of Item 23 for each Lead Teacher, verify documentation, then determine the score, and transfer this score to Column A on the **Summary of Teaching Staff Qualifications Worksheet** on page 64.

6. Determine the average score for Item 23 by summing the individual Lead Teacher scores and dividing by the number of Lead Teachers (the same as the number of groups/classrooms). Record this Item 23 Average Score on the bottom of the **Summary of Teaching Staff Qualifications Worksheet**.

23. Lead Teacher

	1	2	3	4	5	6	7
	Inadequate		Minimal		Good		Excellent

___ 1.1   Lead Teacher does not have an associate degree **or** 60 sh of college credit.

___ 3.1   Lead Teacher has an associate
D   degree **or** has 60 sh of college credit **and** is enrolled in a baccalaureate degree program.

___ 5.1   Lead Teacher has a
D   baccalaureate degree.

___ 7.1   Lead Teacher has a graduate **or**
D   other advanced degree.

___ 1.2   Lead Teacher has less than 12 sh of college credit for ECE/CD coursework.

___ 3.2   Lead Teacher has 21 or more sh
D   of college credit for ECE/CD coursework.

___ 5.2   Lead Teacher has 30 or more sh
D   of college credit for ECE/CD coursework.

___ 7.2   Lead Teacher has certification/
D   licensure required to teach young children in publicly funded pre-K programs.

___ 1.3   Lead Teacher has less than six months experience teaching young children (birth to 8 years of age).[a]

___ 3.3   Lead Teacher has six or more
D   months of experience teaching young children (birth to 8 years of age).[a]

___ 5.3   Lead Teacher has one or more
D   years of experience teaching young children (birth to 8 years of age).[a]

___ 7.3   Lead Teacher has three or more
D   years of experience teaching young children (birth to 8 years of age).[a]

Rationale:

Circle the final score based on the scoring rules on pages 5–6.

1   2   3   4   5   6   7

23. Lead Teacher

24. Teacher (N/A is allowed)

Notes

Teacher refers to a member of the teaching team who shares responsibility with the Lead Teacher for the care and education of an assigned group of children.

Depending on the staffing pattern of the program, there may be more than one person designated as Teacher for each group of children. It is also possible that a group of children will not have someone designated as Teacher on the teaching team.

a To rate 1.2 use the following formula:

❏ It is true, Teacher does not have a CDA.

❏ It is true, Teacher has less than 6 sh of college credit for ECE/CD coursework.

> If both are true, rating is *yes*
> If only one is true, rating is *no*
> If neither is true, rating is *no*

b A *year of experience* is defined as a minimum of 1,200 hours (a six-hour workday for an academic year).

Data Collection Procedures

The information needed to score this item is obtained from data recorded on the **Teaching Staff Qualifications Worksheet** on page 63 for each group/classroom of children.

1. Determine the total number of Teachers for the entire program and duplicate sufficient copies of Item 24 on page 57 so that each individual designated as a Teacher has a separate Item 24 page.

2. Using the information recorded on the **Teaching Staff Qualifications Worksheet**, rate the indicators, verify documentation, and determine the item score(s) for Item 24 for each Teacher.

3. Transfer the individual Teacher Item 24 scores to Column B on the **Summary of Teaching Staff Qualifications Worksheet** on page 64.

4. Determine the average score for Item 24 by summing the individual Teacher scores and dividing by the number of Teachers. Record this Item 24 Average Score on the bottom of the **Summary of Teaching Staff Qualifications Worksheet**.

24. Teacher (N/A is allowed)

	1	2	3	4	5	6	7
	Inadequate		Minimal		Good		Excellent

___ 1.1 Teacher has less than 30 sh of college credit.

___ 3.1 D Teacher has 30 or more sh of college credit.

___ 5.1 D Teacher has an associate degree **or** 60 or more sh of college credit.

___ 7.1 D Teacher has 60 or more sh of college credit **and** is enrolled in a baccalaureate degree program.

___ 1.2 Teacher does not have a CDA credential **or** teacher has less than 6 sh of college credit for ECE/CD coursework.[a]

___ 3.2 D Teacher has a CDA credential plus 6 sh of college credit for ECE/CD coursework **or** 12 or more sh of college credit for ECE/CD coursework.

___ 5.2 D Teacher has 21 or more sh of college credit for ECE/CD coursework.

___ 7.2 D Teacher has 30 or more sh of college credit for ECE/CD coursework.

___ 1.3 Teacher has less than six months experience teaching young children (birth to 8 years of age).[b]

___ 3.3 D Teacher has six months or more of experience teaching young children (birth to 8 years of age).[b]

___ 5.3 D Teacher has one or more years of experience teaching young children (birth to 8 years of age).[b]

___ 7.3 D Teacher has two or more years of experience teaching young children (birth to 8 years of age).[b]

Rationale:

Circle the final score based on the scoring rules on pages 5–6.

1   2   3   4   5   6   7   N/A

24. Teacher

25. Assistant Teacher/Aide (N/A is allowed)

Notes

Assistant Teacher/Aide refers to a member of the teaching team assigned to a group of children who works under the direct supervision of the Lead Teacher and/or Teacher.

Depending on the staffing pattern of the program, there may be more than one person designated as Assistant Teacher/Aide for each group or classroom of children. It is also possible that a group or classroom of children will not have any assigned Assistant Teachers/Aides.

a To rate 1.2 use the following formula:

❏ It is true, Assistant Teacher/Aide has no college credit for ECE/CD coursework.

❏ It is true, Assistant Teacher/Aide is not enrolled in ECE/CD college coursework or CDA training.

> If both are true, rating is *yes*
> If only one is true, rating is *no*
> If neither is true, rating is *no*

b A *year of experience* is defined as a minimum of 1,200 hours (a six-hour workday for an academic year).

Data Collection Procedures

The information needed to score this item is obtained from data recorded on the **Teaching Staff Qualifications Worksheet** on page 63 for each group/classroom of children.

1. Determine the total number of Assistant Teachers/Aides for the entire program and duplicate sufficient copies of Item 25 on page 59 so that each individual designated as an Assistant Teacher/Aide has a separate Item 25 page.

2. Using the information recorded on the **Teaching Staff Qualifications Worksheet**, rate the indicators, verify documentation, and determine the item score(s) for Item 25 for each Assistant Teacher/Aide.

3. Transfer the individual Assistant Teacher/Aide Item 25 scores to Column C on the **Summary of Teaching Staff Qualifications Worksheet** on page 64.

4. Determine the average score for Item 25 by summing the individual Assistant Teacher/Aide scores and dividing by the number of Assistant Teachers/Aides. Record this Item 25 Average Score on the bottom of the **Summary of Teaching Staff Qualifications Worksheet**.

25. Assistant Teacher/Aide (N/A is allowed)

	1	2	3	4	5	6	7
	Inadequate		**Minimal**		**Good**		**Excellent**

___ 1.1 Assistant Teacher/Aide does not have a high school diploma or GED.

___ 3.1 D Assistant Teacher/Aide has a high school diploma or GED.

___ 5.1 D Assistant Teacher/Aide has 9 or more sh of college credit.

___ 7.1 D Assistant Teacher/Aide has 15 or more sh of college credit.

___ 1.2 Assistant Teacher/Aide has no college credit for ECE/CD coursework **and** is not enrolled in ECE/CD college coursework or CDA training.[a]

___ 3.2 D Assistant Teacher/Aide has some college credit for ECE/CD coursework **or** is enrolled in ECE/CD college coursework/CDA training.

___ 5.2 D Assistant Teacher/Aide has 6 or more sh of college credit for ECE/CD coursework **or** has CDA credential.

___ 7.2 D Assistant Teacher/Aide has 9 or more sh of college credit for ECE/CD coursework **or** has a CDA credential plus 3 or more sh of college credit for ECE/CD coursework.

___ 1.3 Assistant Teacher/Aide does not have six or more months of supervised experience teaching young children (birth to 8 years of age).[b]

___ 3.3 D Assistant Teacher/Aide has six or more months of supervised experience teaching young children (birth to 8 years of age).[b]

___ 5.3 D Assistant Teacher/Aide has one or more years of supervised experience teaching young children (birth to 8 years age).[b]

___ 7.3 D Assistant Teacher/Aide has two or more years of supervised experience teaching young children (birth to 8 years of age).[b]

Rationale:

Circle the final score based on the scoring rules on pages 5–6.

1   2   3   4   5   6   7   N/A

25. Assistant Teacher/Aide

Worksheets and Forms

- **Administrator Qualifications Worksheet**

- **Teaching Staff Qualifications Worksheet**

- **Summary of Teaching Staff Qualifications Worksheet**

- **Program Administration Scale (PAS) Item Summary**

- **Program Administration Scale (PAS) Profile**

Administrator Qualifications Worksheet

The Administrator is the individual who has primary responsibility for planning, implementing, and evaluating the early childhood program. The Administrator must be located on-site if the center has four or more classrooms or a total enrollment of 60 or more full-time equivalent (FTE) children. Role titles for the Administrator vary and may include director, manager, coordinator, or principal.

Program: _____ Administrator's name: _____

Highest Education Level	☐ High School/GED ☐ Associate degree ☐ Baccalaureate degree ☐ Graduate degree ☐ Doctorate
General Education	_____ Total semester hours (sh) of college coursework

Specialized ECE/CD Coursework	_____ Total semester hours of ECE/CD coursework
Specialized Coursework in Administration[a]	_____ Total semester hours of coursework in administration
Administrator Credential	Holds administrator credential: ☐ Yes ☐ No Type/level of credential: _____ Issued by: _____

Administrative Experience	_____ years _____ months

[a] *Coursework in administration* refers to content related to one or more of the three domains of the Whole Leadership Framework (Leadership Essentials, Administrative Leadership, Pedagogical Leadership) and **may** include:

Leadership Essentials
- ☐ adult learning theory
- ☐ change management
- ☐ collaboration and team-building
- ☐ cultural competence
- ☐ ethical conduct
- ☐ personal and professional self-awareness
- ☐ oral and written communication
- ☐ organizational climate
- ☐ relational leadership (e.g., creating a trusting and appreciative culture, embedding shared decision-making)
- ☐ systems thinking
- ☐ other _____

Administrative Leadership
- ☐ advocacy
- ☐ fiscal management
- ☐ human resources development
- ☐ legal issues
- ☐ marketing and public relations
- ☐ operations (e.g., systems for risk management, facilities, technology)
- ☐ strategic planning and program evaluation
- ☐ other _____

Pedagogical Leadership
- ☐ application of child development theory and research to practice
- ☐ application of adult learning theory and research to practice
- ☐ coaching and mentoring
- ☐ culturally responsive teaching and leading
- ☐ family engagement (e.g., fostering family leadership, promoting partnerships)
- ☐ reflective supervision
- ☐ use of child assessment data to improve teaching and learning (e.g., cycles of continuous quality improvement)
- ☐ other _____

Teaching Staff Qualifications Worksheet
(Lead Teachers, Teachers, Assistant Teachers/Aides)

Please complete one worksheet for each group/classroom (see instructions on pages 54, 56, and 58).

Program: _____ Group/classroom: _____

Teaching staff initials: ____ ____ ____ ____

Teaching role*: ____ ____ ____ ____

---

* Teaching Roles:

Lead Teacher (LT)
The individual with the highest professional qualifications assigned to teach a group of children and who is responsible for daily lesson planning, parent conferences, child assessment, and curriculum planning.

Teacher (T)
A member of the teaching team who shares responsibility with the Lead Teacher for the care and education of an assigned group of children.

Assistant Teacher/Aide (ATA)
A member of the teaching team assigned to a group of children who works under the direct supervision of the Lead Teacher and/or Teacher.

Highest Education Level

	☐	☐	☐	☐
High School/GED	☐	☐	☐	☐
Associate degree	☐	☐	☐	☐
Baccalaureate degree	☐	☐	☐	☐
Graduate degree	☐	☐	☐	☐
Doctorate degree	☐	☐	☐	☐

General Education

Total semester hours (sh) of completed college coursework ____ ____ ____ ____

Currently enrolled in a bachelor's degree program ☐ ☐ ☐ ☐

Specialized Coursework

Total semester hours of completed ECE/CD coursework ____ ____ ____ ____

Currently enrolled in ECE/CD college coursework ☐ ☐ ☐ ☐

Credentials

CDA ☐ ☐ ☐ ☐

State Teacher Certification/Licensure ☐ ☐ ☐ ☐

Teaching Experience

years ____ ____ ____ ____

months ____ ____ ____ ____

Summary of Teaching Staff Qualifications Worksheet

Program: _____   Date: _____

	Group/Classroom Name	A Lead Teacher Item 23 Score	B Teacher Item 24 Score	C Assistant Teacher Item 25 Score
1.	_____	_____	_____ _____ _____	_____ _____ _____
2.	_____	_____	_____ _____	_____ _____
3.	_____	_____	_____ _____	_____ _____
4.	_____	_____	_____ _____ _____	_____ _____ _____
5.	_____	_____	_____ _____	_____ _____ _____

Sum of scores in Column A		Sum of scores in Column B		Sum of scores in Column C	
	÷		÷		÷
Number of scores in Column A		Number of scores in Column B		Number of scores in Column C	
	=		=		=
Item 23 Average Score		Item 24 Average Score		Item 25 Average Score	

64

Program Administration Scale (PAS) Item Summary

Program: _____   Date: _____

Instructions

Use this form to summarize the item scores and to calculate the Total PAS Score and Average PAS Item Score.

- ◆ Enter the item scores in the spaces provided

- ◆ Sum all the item scores and enter the total in the space provided. This is the Total PAS Score.

- ◆ Divide the Total PAS Score by the total number of items (minimum of 21 for all programs; 22, 23, 24, or 25 depending on whether or not the program has scored items 11, 12, 24, and 25 as N/A). The resulting number is the Average PAS Score.

Item   Score

1. Hiring and Orientation   _____
2. Supervision and Performance Appraisal   _____
3. Staff Development and Professional Growth   _____
4. Compensation   _____
5. Benefits   _____
6. Staffing Patterns and Scheduling   _____
7. Facilities   _____
8. Risk Management   _____
9. Marketing and Public Relations   _____
10. Technology   _____
11. Screening and Identification (N/A is allowed)   _____
12. Assessment in Support of Learning (N/A is allowed) _____
13. Budget Planning   _____
14. Accounting Practices   _____
15. Strategic Planning   _____
16. Evaluation and Continuous Improvement   _____
17. Family Communications   _____
18. Family Support and Engagment   _____
19. Community Outreach   _____
20. Meetings and Shared Decision-Making   _____
21. Internal Communications   _____
22. Administrator   _____
23. Lead Teacher   _____
24. Teacher (N/A is allowed)   _____
25. Assistant Teacher/Aide (N/A is allowed)   _____

Sum of Item Scores   [   ] ÷ [   ] = [   ]

Total PAS Score	Number of Items Scored	Average PAS Item Score

Program Administration Scale (PAS) Profile

Program: _____ **Date:** _____

Subscales	Items	1	2	3	4	5	6	7
Human Resources	1. Hiring and Orientation							
	2. Supervision and Performance Appraisal							
	3. Staff Development and Professional Growth							
Personnel Cost and Allocation	4. Compensation							
	5. Benefits							
	6. Staffing Patterns and Scheduling							
Operations	7. Facilities							
	8. Risk Management							
	9. Marketing and Public Relations							
	10. Technology							
Screening and Assessment	11. Screening and Identification (N/A is allowed)							
	12. Assessment in Support of Learning (N/A is allowed)							
Fiscal Management	13. Budget Planning							
	14. Accounting Practices							
Organizational Growth and Development	15. Strategic Planning							
	16. Evaluation and Continuous Improvement							
Family and Community Partnerships	17. Family Communications							
	18. Family Support and Engagement							
	19. Community Outreach							
Relational Leadership	20. Meetings and Shared Decision-Making							
	21. Internal Communications							
Staff Qualifications	22. Administrator							
	23. Lead Teacher							
	24. Teacher (N/A is allowed)							
	25. Assistant Teacher/Aide (N/A is allowed)							

Total PAS Score _____ ÷ **Number of items** _____ = **Average PAS Item Score** _____

P
A
S

Appendices

- **Psychometric Characteristics**

- **References and Resources**

Psychometric Characteristics

Psychometric Criteria

The development of the *Program Administration Scale* was guided by seven psychometric criteria:

1. The PAS should measure distinct but related administrative practices of an early childhood program.

2. The PAS should be able to differentiate low- and high-quality programs.

3. The PAS should be applicable for use in different types of program (e.g., for-profit, nonprofit, part-day, full-day, faith-based, military, Head Start, state Pre-K).

4. The PAS should be applicable for use in programs of varying sizes.

5. The PAS should demonstrate good internal consistency among scale items.

6. The PAS should demonstrate good inter-rater reliability.

7. The PAS should be easy to score and generate an easy-to-understand profile to support program improvement efforts.

Normative Samples

Three reliability and validity studies of the *Program Administration Scale* have been conducted by the authors. Sample #1 included data collected in 2003 from 67 center-based early care and education programs in Illinois. Sample #2 included data collected between 2006 and 2009 from 564 centers in 25 states. Sample #3 was collected using the second edition of the PAS between 2011 and 2020 and included 693 centers representing 31 states and Washington DC.

Sample #1. The Illinois Network of Child Care Resource and Referral Agencies (INCCRRA) generated a list of all child care centers in Cook (Chicago), Cook (Suburban), Jackson, Madison, McLean, and Winnebago counties with contact information and descriptive data on center capacity, NAEYC-accreditation status, and legal auspices. The counties targeted for this sample were selected because they included urban, suburban, and rural geographic regions of the state.

The Metropolitan Chicago Information Center (MCIC) took the INCCRRA information and constructed a sample frame based on the center's NAEYC-accreditation status (non-accredited and accredited) and center size (small, medium, large). From a pool of 176 programs that provided adequate representation of each of the state's geographic areas, 124 centers were randomly contacted and asked to participate in a reliability and validity study of the PAS. A total of 67 centers agreed to participate and interviews with the on-site administrator were scheduled.

The mean licensed capacity of centers included in Sample #1 was 102 children. Centers employed on average 17 staff who worked more than ten hours per week. Thirty-two of the centers (48%) were accredited by the National Association for the Education of Young Children (NAEYC). Approximately two-thirds of the programs (67%) were nonprofit; one-third represented the for-profit sector. Twenty-two of the nonprofit programs received Head Start funding and five programs were sponsored by faith-based organizations.

Sample #2. The PAS assessments for Sample #2 were conducted as part of the national PAS assessor certification process. Assessors were trained over a four-day period and achieved an inter-rater reliability of 86% or higher with PAS national anchors. Data for the 564 PAS assessments were collected within four months of completing reliability training. Only PAS data from assessments that met certification review criteria were included.

While data regarding the PAS items were collected on all programs, descriptive background information on some of the centers was not gathered. There is missing data in Sample #2 relating to program size and accreditation status for 12 programs. Information relating to funding sources and program type (legal auspices) were not collected for 68 programs.

The mean licensed capacity of centers included in Sample #2 was 90 children, with the average center caring for 64 children at least 35 hours a week. Centers employed, on average, 14 staff who worked more than ten hours per week. Approximately two-thirds of the programs (69%) were nonprofit; the remaining programs represented the for-profit sector. Thirty-five percent of programs in Sample #2 received Head Start funding, 36% received state pre-kindergarten funding, and 23% were affiliated with faith-based organizations.

Sample #3. The PAS assessments for Sample #3 were conducted as part of the national PAS assessor certification process between 2011 and 2020. Assessors were trained on the second edition of the PAS over a five-day period and achieved inter-rater reliability of 86% or higher with PAS national anchors. Data for the PAS assessments were collected within four months of completing reliability training. Only PAS data from assessments that met certification review criteria were included.

The PAS data for Sample #3 included 693 center-based programs representing 31 states and the District of Columbia. While data regarding the PAS items were collected on all programs, descriptive background information on some of the centers was not gathered. There was missing data in Sample #3 relating to program size for one program, NAEYC accreditation status for two programs, and program type (legal auspice) for 15 programs.

Programs ranged in licensed capacity from 8 to 430 with a mean licensed capacity of 92 and a median licensed capacity of 78. On average, centers had 54 children enrolled full-day and 24 children enrolled part-day. Centers employed, on average, 15 staff who worked more than ten hours per week. Thirteen percent of programs in Sample #3 received Head Start funding, 22% received state prekindergarten funding, and 19% were affiliated with faith-based organizations. Just over half of the programs (55%) were nonprofit and 43% represented the for-profit sector.

Table 1 provides a distribution of the centers in Sample #3 by size and NAEYC accreditation status. Table 2 provides a distribution of the sample by program type (legal auspices).

Table 1

Distribution of Centers by Size and NAEYC Accreditation Status–Sample #3 (n = 691)

Accreditation Status	Center Size						Total	
	Small		Medium		Large			
	n	%	*n*	%	*n*	%	*n*	%
Not Accredited	183	83	200	84	204	87	587	85
Accredited	37	17	37	16	30	13	104	15
Total	**220**	**100**	**237**	**100**	**234**	**100**	**691**	**100**

Note: Small = licensed for less than 60 children; medium = licensed for 60–100 children; large = licensed for more than 100 children.

Table 2

Distribution of Centers by Program Type–Sample #3 (n = 678)

Program Type	n	%
Nonprofit	**382**	**56.3**
Nonprofit—college or university affiliated	27	4.0
Nonprofit—private affiliated with a social service agency or hospital	63	9.3
Nonprofit—private independent	217	32.0
Nonprofit—public sponsored by federal, state, or local government	62	9.1
Nonprofit—public school	13	1.9
For-profit	**296**	**43.7**
For-profit—private proprietary or partnership	224	33.0
For-profit—corporation or chain (e.g., KinderCare, La Petite Academy)	64	9.4
For-profit—corporate sponsored (e.g., Bright Horizons)	8	1.3
Total	**678**	**100**

Reliability and Validity

Content validity. Content validity for the *Program Administration Scale* was initially established in 2003 by a panel of ten early childhood experts who evaluated each indicator, item, and subscale on the PAS to ensure that key leadership and management practices of center-based early childhood programs were included. Content reviewers were asked to respond to the following questions and provide feedback:

- Do the items under each subscale adequately describe the subscale?

- Do the indicators under each item adequately represent each item?

- Do the indicators appropriately show increasing levels of quality on a continuum?

- Does the wording of the item and subscale headings adequately reflect their content?

In addition to the content evaluation by ten early childhood experts, the *Program Administration Scale* was also reviewed informally by ten other early childhood administrators, consultants, and trainers. Multiple refinements were made to the wording and layout of the PAS as a result of the helpful feedback received from reviewers. Redundant indicators were deleted and the data-collection protocol was streamlined.

Since the publication of the first edition of the PAS in 2004 and the second edition in 2011, additional refinements have been made to the Additional Notes accompanying the PAS indicators based on feedback received from assessors who have visited programs and interviewed administrators as part of PAS assessments in different regions of the country. This helped ensure that the indicators continue to reflect quality leadership practices in early care and education.

Descriptive statistics. Table 3 provides the mean scores and standard deviations for the 25 items scored using the 7-point scale of the PAS second edition. There were a total of 81 indicator strands rated to compute scores for the 25 items.

Table 3

Mean Scores and Standard Deviations for PAS Items by Subscale–
Sample #3 (N = 693)

Item #	Item	Indicator Strands	*M*	*SD*
Human Resources Development				
1	Staff orientation	3	3.32	2.04
2	Supervision and performance appraisal	3	3.23	2.05
3	Staff development	3	3.56	2.22
Personnel Cost and Allocation				
4	Compensation	3	2.22	1.78
5	Benefits	5	1.61	1.36
6	Staffing patterns and scheduling	4	3.17	2.06
Center Operations				
7	Facilities management	3	4.65	2.28
8	Risk management	4	3.01	1.98
9	Internal communications	5	2.19	1.80
Child Assessment				
10	Screening and identification of special needs	3	3.65	2.55
11	Assessment in support of learning	2	4.18	2.37
Fiscal Management				
12	Budget planning	3	3.46	2.33
13	Accounting practices	3	3.23	2.33
Program Planning and Evaluation				
14	Program evaluation	3	2.89	2.28
15	Strategic planning	2	2.45	2.12
Family Partnerships				
16	Family communications	4	3.54	2.22
17	Family support and involvement	3	5.19	1.71
Marketing and Public Relations				
18	External communications	3	4.29	1.75
19	Community outreach	3	3.73	2.10
Technology				
20	Technological resources	2	6.44	1.35
21	Use of technology	3	4.13	2.04
Staff Qualifications				
22	Administrator	5	2.35	1.59
23	Lead Teacher[a]	3	2.64	1.46
24	Teacher[b]	3	2.66	1.84
25	Assistant Teacher/Aide[c]	3	2.75	2.01
	Total PAS	**81**	**84.53**	**49.59**

Note: [a] *n* = 3,460. [b] *n* = 1,900. [c] *n* = 2,015.

The Total PAS Score represented in Table 3 is the sum of the item mean scores. Because the 10 subscales of the PAS were used only as convenient headings for clustering items, and not as separate indicators of organizational effectiveness, mean scores for the subscales were not included on the profile that users generate to guide their program improvement efforts.

The Average PAS Item Score for Sample #3 was 3.40 with a median score of 3.32 and standard deviation of 1.12. The skewness and kurtosis for Sample #3 Average PAS Item Score was .31 and -.63, respectively, well within the acceptable ranges (-2 and +2) for demonstrating a normal univariate distribution. Further, visual representations of the data indicated that the data used for Sample #3 represent a relatively normal distribution of scores and a bell-shaped graph with the majority of the data symmetrical and centered around the mean.

When looking at the national norms for Sample #3 detailed in Table 3, it should be noted that the percentage of NAEYC-accredited programs in this sample (15%) is more than double that of the overall national percentage of accredited programs, which is 6%. The Total PAS Score and individual item mean scores reflect this concentration of higher-quality programs.

Because the data came from assessments collected as part of the PAS assessor certification process, most of the programs participating in Sample #1, Sample #2, and Sample #3 did not receive a copy of the instrument prior to the administration of the scale. This undoubtedly lowers the Total PAS Score and the Average PAS Item Score for each sample. In the real-world application of the PAS (e.g., as used in quality rating and improvement systems), program administrators have access to the tool prior to its administration, are better prepared with the documentation needed, and therefore the percentage of programs being rated at a level 1 on items is decreased.

Internal consistency. The degree of coherence of items included on the *Program Administration Scale*, its internal consistency, was determined through computation of Cronbach's Alpha coefficient. Coefficient alpha for the total scale was .85 for Sample #1, .86 for Sample #2, and .90 for Sample #3, indicating that the PAS has established and maintained strong internal consistency among items.

Distinctiveness of the subscales. The 10 subscales were correlated to determine the extent to which they measured distinct, though somewhat related, aspects of early childhood administration. Subscale intercorrelations for Sample #1 ranged from .09 to .63. Subscale intercorrelations for Sample #2 ranged from .04 to .72. Subscale data for Sample #3 ranged from .23 to .61. These analyses confirm that the subscales, for the most part, measure distinct characteristics of organizational administration. Table 4 reports the results of the Pearson's *r* correlational analysis for Sample #3.

Table 4

Subscale Intercorrelations–Sample #3

Subscale	2	3	4	5	6	7	8	9	10
1. Human Resources Development	.45*	.61*	.54*	.42*	.60*	.53*	.48*	.42*	.28*
2. Personnel Cost and Allocation	-	.48*	.49*	.48*	.48*	.50*	.40*	.37*	.36*
3. Center Operations		-	.45*	.40*	.55*	.51*	.45*	.40*	.34*
4. Child Assessment			-	.38*	.46*	.60*	.39*	.36*	.41*
5. Fiscal Management				-	.49*	.41*	.44*	.33*	.28*
6. Program Planning and Evaluation					-	.53*	.46*	.35*	.35*
7. Family Partnerships						-	.49*	.38*	.44*
8. Marketing and Public Relations							-	.37*	.27*
9. Technology								-	.23*
10. Staff Qualifications									-

Note: * = *p* < .001

Item intercorrelations were also calculated using Pearson's *r*. These coefficients ranged from .02 to .78 for Sample #1, .01 to .58 for Sample #2, and .04 to .62 for Sample #3, confirming that the individual items on the PAS measure somewhat distinct but related characteristics of organizational administration.

Inter-rater reliability. Inter-rater reliability, the degree to which the assessor's item scores match the PAS anchor's scores, was determined during a five-day training on the use of the instrument. Using a videotape of the entire interview protocol, assessors were rated on how often they matched the PAS anchor's scores within 1 point for each item. Inter-rater reliability for all certified PAS assessors gathering data was 86% or higher.

Differentiating programs. In order to determine if the *Program Administration Scale* adequately differentiates programs of varying quality, an independent *t*-test and analysis of variance procedures were employed. NAEYC accreditation status was used as a measure of program quality. NAEYC-accredited programs were presumed to be of higher quality than those that were not accredited. First, an independent *t*-test was used to explore differences in Average PAS Item Scores between accredited and not accredited programs in Sample #3. Results indicated higher Average PAS Item Scores in accredited programs ($M = 4.10$, $SD = 1.01$) compared to not accredited programs ($M = 3.27$, $SD = 1.09$). This difference was significant at $t(690) = -7.30$, $p = .000$ and represented a large effect size ($d = .80$). Table 5 shows the six items on which NAEYC-accredited programs scored the highest.

Table 5

Highest Scoring PAS Items for NAEYC Accredited Programs—Sample #3 (N = 105)

Item	Accredited	
	M	SD
Technological Resources	6.69	1.14
Family Support and Involvement	6.04	1.41
Assessment in Support of Learning	5.39	1.95
Facilities Management	5.26	2.09
Family Communications	4.82	1.90
External Communications	4.66	1.62

ANOVA results further supported the notion that the PAS can distinguish between program quality by comparing the Total PAS Score between accredited and not accredited programs. Programs from Sample #3 that were accredited also had significantly higher Total PAS Scores than those that were not accredited ($M = 94.54$, $SD = 23.67$; $M = 76.30$, $SD = 25.73$), $F(1,690) = 45.85$, $p = .000$. Similar results were found in the analyses of Sample #1 ($M = 92.12$ versus $M = 72.06$) and Sample #2 ($M = 85.68$, versus $M = 73.18$). The Total PAS Scores for these ANOVAs were based on 23 items (possible total score range 23–161), since all centers did not include the positions of Teacher and Assistant Teacher/Aide as part of the teaching staff. Taken together, these results provide confirmatory evidence that the PAS can adequately differentiate programs based on level of quality.

An ANOVA was also used to determine whether programs of varying sizes scored differently on the *Program Administration Scale*. An analysis of the Sample #1 data found that for 23 of the 25 items, there were no statistically significant differences based on program size (small, medium, large). The results for Sample #2 were somewhat different, indicating that there were significant differences in Total PAS Scores based on program size with large programs ($M = 83.57$) and medium-size programs ($M = 77.06$), scoring significantly higher on

the overall PAS than small programs ($M = 74.03$, $F = 5.77$, $p < .01$). Results for Sample #3 were more closely aligned with those from Sample #1 and showed no significant effect of program size on Total PAS Score for small ($M = 81.85$, $SD = 25.84$), medium ($M = 80.51$, $SD = 26.69$), or large ($M = 85.92$, $SD = 29.23$) programs, $F(2,689) = 2.51$, $p = .08$. Additionally there were no significant differences found for Average PAS Item Score for small ($M = 3.38$, $SD = 1.05$), medium ($M = 3.30$, $SD = 1.10$), or large ($M = 3.51$, $SD = 1.12$) programs, $F(2,689) = 2.02$, $p = .14$. These findings support the premise that the PAS does not show bias based on program size.

Analyses were also conducted on Sample #3 to determine how other program characteristics may impact Average PAS Item Score. Specifically, the data were examined to determine the potential effects of Head Start funding, state prekindergarten funding, and program type (legal auspice) on average scores.

Results from an independent *t*-test showed a significant difference in Average PAS Item Scores between programs that received Head Start funding ($M = 4.04$, $SD = 1.13$) and those that did not ($M = 3.30$, $SD = 1.09$), $t(691) = - 6.05$, $p = .000$. This represented a medium effect size ($d = .66$).

An independent *t*-test was also used to explore whether programs that received state prekindergarten funding showed a significant difference in Average PAS Item Scores than programs that did not receive state prekindergarten funding. Results indicated that Average PAS Item Scores did vary significantly, with state-funded prekindergarten programs scoring higher, on average ($M = 3.95$, $SD = 1.05$), than programs not receiving the funding ($M = 3.24$, $SD = 1.09$), $t(691) = - 7.06$, $p = .000$. This represented a medium effect size ($d = .65$).

Finally, a *t*-test was again used to determine whether Average PAS Item Scores differed by program type (legal auspice). Results revealed that nonprofit programs had significantly higher Average PAS Item Scores ($M = 3.68$, $SD = 1.07$) than for-profit programs ($M = 3.05$; $SD = 1.09$), $t(676) = -7.57$, $p = .000$. This difference represented a medium effect size ($d = .59$).

Concurrent validity. Concurrent validity for the PAS was determined by a correlational analysis with two other instruments that measure early childhood organizational effectiveness: the Professional Growth subscale of the *Early Childhood Work Environment Survey* (ECWES) and the Parents and Staff subscale of the *Early Childhood Environment Rating Scale–Revised*. As Table 6 shows, the moderate correlations with both the ECERS-R Parents and Staff subscale and ECWES Professional Growth subscale indicate that the PAS measures related but not redundant characteristics of organizational quality.

Table 6

Correlation of PAS Subscales with the ECERS-R Parents and Staff Subscale and the ECWES Professional Growth Subscale– Sample #1 (N = 67)

PAS Subscale	ECERS-R	ECWES
Human Resources Development	.33	.42
Personnel Cost and Allocation	.45	.42
Center Operations	.33	.32
Child Assessment	.29	.05
Fiscal Management	.47	.40
Program Planning and Evaluation	.36	.24
Family Partnerships	.34	.43
Marketing and Public Relations	.10	.05
Technology	.32	.38
Staff Qualifications	.26	.35
PAS Total	**.53**	**.52**

The results of the reliability and validity study support the conclusion that the *Program Administration Scale* has achieved all seven psychometric criteria: It measures somewhat distinct but related administrative practices of early childhood programs; can differentiate between low- and high-quality programs as measured by NAEYC accreditation status; is applicable for use in different types of programs; can be used by programs of varying sizes; demonstrates good internal consistency; has good inter-rater reliability; and is easy to score and use as a tool to support program quality improvement efforts.

Related Research

The *Program Administration Scale* has been used in numerous studies evaluating the quality of center-based administrative practices, statewide quality rating and improvement systems, and state professional development and director credentialing systems. The following are selected studies that provide evidence of the predictive validity of the PAS and confirm the utility of the instrument for measuring quality, monitoring improvements, and benchmarking change in organizational practices.

Study #1. Lower and Cassidy (2007) conducted a study of 30 centers in North Carolina to assess the relationship among program administration practices, staff's perceptions of organizational climate, and classroom quality. The PAS was used to assess the quality of administrative practices; the *Early Childhood Work Environment Survey* (ECWES) was used to measure organizational climate; and observations of two classrooms at each center using the *Early Childhood Environment Rating Scale–R* (ECERS) were conducted to assess the quality of the classroom learning environment.

Internal consistency for the PAS was .88. Mean item scores ranged from 2.87 to 5.19. Internal consistency of the ECERS-R was .83; scores ranged from 3.90 to 6.00. The results of the data analysis found a dynamic relationship among program leadership and management practices, teachers' perceptions of their work environment reflected in its organizational climate, and how those variables relate to the classroom practices experienced by children.

Program administration, as measured by the PAS, was significantly related to classroom global quality. The Pearson's r correlation revealed a statistically significant moderate correlation between PAS scores and ECERS-R scores ($r = .29$, $p < .05$). The researchers also found that directors with a four-year degree scored significantly higher on the PAS ($M = 3.24$) than directors without a four-year degree ($M = 2.49$). The study suggests that program administration practices and organizational climate are important variables related to the quality of classroom learning environments.

Study #2. The McCormick Center for Early Childhood Leadership (MCECL) at National Louis University, in collaboration with the Chicago Department of Family and Suport Services, conducted a study to examine how administrative practices in Head Start programs are related to classroom quality (MCECL, 2010b). The research also looked at director qualifications in Head Start programs to understand how specific dimensions of director qualifications are related to the quality of Head Start administrative practices and the quality of the classroom learning environment. The PAS was used as a measure of the quality of administrative practices and the ECERS-R was used as a measure of classroom quality. Data were collected in 2006 in 452 Head Start classrooms in 138 centers in Chicago.

Multiple regression analyses, controlling for length of day, number of teachers, annual turnover rate, lead teacher qualifications, and child enrollment, were conducted to understand whether higher PAS scores predicted higher ECERS-R scores. Mean PAS scores for this sample were calculated at 3.42, with scores ranging from 1.58 to 5.88, while mean ECERS-R scores were calculated at 4.20, with scores ranging from 2.41 to 6.12. The results of the data analysis revealed that administrative quality accounted for 26% of the variance in Head Start classroom quality ($t = 3.62$, $p = .0001$), demonstrating that administrative practices, as measured by the PAS, strongly influenced the quality of care that children receive in their classrooms.

To address the second research question regarding director qualifications, an overall PAS score was calculated using all PAS items except staff qualifications. Correlations were then conducted between the different dimensions of director qualifications and PAS scores. Correlations revealed that higher-quality administrative practices were associated with directors who had a master's degree ($r = .22$, $p < .01$), had completed more management coursework ($r = .20$, $p < .01$), and had made more professional contributions during the past three years ($r = .25$, $p < .01$).

Finally, the researchers looked specifically at the relationship between directors' qualifications, as measured by the PAS, and classroom quality, as measured by the ECERS-R. The results of the data analysis found that higher classroom quality was associated with directors who had a bachelor's degree or higher ($r = .22$, $p < .01$), had completed 24 or more semester hours of early childhood coursework ($r = .19$, $p = .02$), and had made at least four professional contributions during the past three years ($r = .20$, $p = .01$).

Study #3. In 2006, researchers at the National Center for Children and Families at Teachers College, Columbia University were commissioned to propose a uniform and comprehensive performance measurement system for all publicly funded early childhood programs in New York City (Kagan et al., 2008). Two of the measures used in the citywide pilot were the PAS and the ECERS-R. The total sample included 130 classrooms from 37 Head Start, community-based child care, and universal prekindergarten programs.

The Average PAS Item Scores for the 35 sites that completed a PAS assessment was 3.87. Scores ranged from 2.28 to 5.28. Head Start programs in the sample scored highest with an Average PAS Item Score of 4.59. Community-based child care programs scored lowest with an Average PAS Item Score of 3.34. Results of the data analysis showed a correlation between the PAS and the ECERS-R scores ($r = .52, p < .01$).

To assure that the two measures capture distinct dimensions of quality, factor analysis was employed. Two major factors emerged from the analysis. The first factor exclusively included items from the ECERS-R, while the second only included items from the PAS, indicating that these two instruments capture distinct elements of program quality. The researchers' recommendation was that New York City's unified performance measurement system should use both measures; program administration and classroom quality are both important elements of a well-functioning program.

Study #4. An evaluation of Arkansas's professional development support system was conducted by KeyStone Research Corporation using the PAS as one of the tools to measure the quality of centers that had received professional development support through Arkansas State University Childhood Services (Miller & Bogatova, 2007). Trained PAS assessors gathered data from 169 early care and education programs.

The results of the evaluation showed that the PAS differentiated the quality of administrative practices between programs classified as meeting minimal licensing requirements, those that met the state accreditation standards classified as Arkansas Quality Approval (QA) programs, and those that met state prekindergarten standards classified as Arkansas Better Chance (ABC) programs. In 24 of the 25 PAS items, QA and ABC programs outperformed programs classified as meeting minimum licensing standards. The Average PAS Item Score for the QA and/or ABC programs was 4.47, compared to 3.12 for those programs classified as meeting minimum licensing requirements ($p < .001$). The study also found statistically significant differences in PAS item scores between nonprofit and for-profit programs ($p < .001$).

Study #5. The McCormick Center for Early Childhood Leadership conducted a study to examine the early childhood program characteristics associated with utilization of the Illinois Great START (Strategies to Attract and Retain Teachers) wage supplement initiative (MCECL, 2007). Forty Illinois Department of Human Services (IDHS) site-contracted early care and education centers were included in the sample: 20 that had a high utilization of Great START funds and 20 that did not use or had a low utilization of these funds. The ECERS-R was used to measure the quality of 70 preschool classrooms in the sample; the PAS was used to measure the quality of leadership and management practices of the 40 programs included in the study.

The results of the data analysis revealed that in preschool classrooms, notable differences in the level of program quality were found as measured by the ECERS-R. Those centers classified as high utilization of Great START funds consistently demonstrated higher-quality teaching practices ($p < .05$). In 22 of the 25 PAS items, the Total PAS Score and the Average PAS Item Score, there were notable differences in the quality of administrative practices between those centers classified as high versus low utilization of Great START funds. Those classified as high utilization consistently demonstrated higher leadership and management practices. Statistically significant differences ($p < .05$) were found between the two groups in five items: Compensation, Screening and Identification of Special Needs, Strategic Planning, Lead Teacher Qualifications, and Assistant Teacher/Aide Qualifications.

Study #6. Researchers at the Human Development Institute at the University of Kentucky conducted a study to assess the impact of the Kentucky Professional Development Framework on classroom quality and child outcomes (Rous et al., 2008). The PAS was one of several different instruments used to collect data and inform the researchers and state policymakers about the effectiveness of the professional development system and the organizational factors that support or impede quality practices. The sample included 227 programs including Head Start, child care, and public prekindergarten.

In looking at the specific factors that impact early childhood professionals' ability to participate in professional development activities, the researchers found that administrators who worked with teachers who utilized Professional Development Plans as part of the state's Professional Development Framework scored significantly higher on the PAS item Staff Development ($t = 2.67$, $p < .01$). Teachers felt more supported by their administrator when they used Professional Development Plans. The researchers conclude that a supportive administrator combined with teacher experience and education, the use of Professional Development Plans by teachers, and the number of self-selected trainings attended by teachers had the highest impact on classroom quality scores as measured by the ECERS-R and the *Early Language and Literacy Classroom Observation* (ELLCO).

The results of the data analysis also surfaced statistically significant relationships between the PAS item Staff Development and the ELLCO Literacy Environment Checklist ($r = .28$, $p < .01$) and the average ECERS-R score ($r = .20$, $p < .05$). A similar significant relationship surfaced between the PAS item Supervision and Performance Appraisal and the ELLCO Literacy Environment Checklist ($r = .20$, $p < .05$) and the average ECERS-R score ($r = .20$, $p < .05$).

Study #7. Launched in 2008, the Tennessee Early Childhood Program Administrator Credential (TECPAC) is the recognition awarded to center directors who have demonstrated specific competencies for effective leadership and management through formal academics, experience, and portfolio assessment. Each year the Tennessee State University's Center of Excellence for Learning Sciences conducts an evaluation of the credential. The PAS is used as a pre- and post-assessment to measure changes in program quality

for the administrators who are awarded the credential. (The Staff Qualifications subscale is not included in the evaluation data as that information is gathered elsewhere.)

The results of the 2009–10 evaluation demonstrated that 93% of the credential completers and 100% of the credential specialists felt the PAS was a beneficial tool for supporting program growth. Changes in mean item scores ranged from .02 (Benefits) to 3.00 points (Staff Orientation) with a mean item improvement of 1.81 points. The most significant changes were related to the topics included in the credential training (Mietlicki, 2010).

Study #8. Researchers at the University of Arkansas's Partners for Inclusive Communities conducted an assessment of the state's Better Beginnings Quality Rating and Improvement System (McKelvey et al., 2010). The PAS is one of the required assessments used in Better Beginnings to achieve a quality rating. The four PAS items that comprise the Staff Qualifications subscale are not included in the Better Beginnings QRIS. Also, Item 5 (Benefits) and Item 6 (Staffing Patterns and Scheduling) are assessed but not counted in a program's overall score.

Using data collected as part of the Evaluation of the Arkansas Early Childhood Professional Development System (AECPDS), the evaluation team compared the original scoring with the Better Beginnings scoring of the PAS. They found that the correlations between the Better Beginnings PAS, the Environment Rating Scales, and the Arnett Caregiver Interaction Scales (CIS) were weaker than with the original scoring of the PAS. The original PAS scoring was significantly related to teacher behaviors that support children's cognitive development and school readiness ($p < .01$). The Better Beginnings PAS scoring was not. These behaviors include engaging the children with open-ended questions and encouraging children in the use of symbolic/literacy materials, numbers and spatial concepts, and problem solving. The researchers state that the omitted PAS items may impact the measure's usefulness for Better Beginnings and recommend re-introducing the items that have been excluded from Better Beginnings.

Using the Better Beginnings scoring of the PAS, the evaluation team sought to determine whether cut scores for the system were meaningful. Better Beginnings' Levels 1 and 2 do not require PAS assessments while Level 3 requires a minimum score of 4.00. The researchers found that programs scoring lower than 4.00 on the scale have teachers who are less sensitive, more detached, and less supportive of socio-emotional development, and have classrooms with lower overall global environmental quality ratings.

Study #9. Arend (2010) investigated the human resource management practices of early childhood directors and the relationship between directors' level of management training and the quality of human resource management practices. The study used nine items from the PAS related to human resource issues—Staff Orientation, Staff Development, Supervision and Performance Appraisal, Compensation, Benefits, Staffing Patterns and Scheduling, Internal Communications, Program Evaluation, and Strategic Planning. The sample comprised 965 directors from five states. Data were collected electronically via self-report questionnaire.

The results of the data analysis revealed the strongest management practices in the area of Supervision and Performance Appraisal and the weakest in the areas of Strategic Planning and Benefits. The majority of scores fell in the *minimal* to *good* range with none of the median scale scores greater than *good*.

Significant differences were also found among directors with varying levels of management coursework in six of the nine areas examined. In all of the post-hoc comparisons, directors with more management coursework scored higher than those with fewer management credits. In six of these areas, the differences reached statistical significance ($p < .01$).

Study #10. A study was conducted to discern differences in the quality of classroom learning environments, teacher-child interactions, organizational climate, leadership and management practices, staff turnover, and accreditation status as the result of a comprehensive professional development and quality enhancement initiative. Nine child care centers associated with well-established social service agencies in Chicago participated in the study, which spanned four years. The PAS was the instrument used to assess changes in the quality of leadership and management practices.

The intervention, conducted by the Center for Urban Research and Learning at Loyola University, included on-site technical assistance as well as a variety of professional development supports for teaching and administrative staff at the centers. The results of the data analysis show that there were notable improvements in program quality in the early childhood centers that participated in this project. The centers consistently demonstrated higher-quality teaching practices (as measured by the Environment Rating Scales), a more positive work climate (as measured by the ECWES), and improved leadership and management practices (as measured by the PAS) in 2006 compared to 2002. The centers also experienced a significant decrease in the rate of annual turnover among teaching staff (Bloom & Talan, 2006).

With respect to the PAS, the results of a paired t-test statistical analysis revealed that in five of the ten subscales, the pre–post differences were statistically significant ($p < .05$). In 20 of the 25 PAS items, there were improvements in the quality of administrative practices as measured by the PAS between 2002 and 2006. In 12 of the items, these changes were statistically significant ($p < .05$). The Average PAS Item Score increased from 3.63 in 2002 to 4.72 in 2006 ($p < .05$).

This positive finding, however, masks significant differences in the magnitude of the changes in leadership and management practices at the nine centers. While the Average PAS Item Score increased between 2002 and 2006 at each of the centers assessed, at four of the centers the Average PAS Item Score increased by 33% or more. At one center, the Average PAS Item Score improved by 67%.

Study #11. Quality New York, a NAEYC accreditation facilitation project, is a comprehensive program improvement model that includes two types of support for participating programs—group support activities and individualized on-site support. In an effort to better understand the impact of support on the quality of early childhood classroom and administrative practices, the Center for Assessment and Policy Development collected data from 11 early care and education programs that had participated in the Quality New York project for at least 18 months and had been identified as having substantial weaknesses (Stephens, 2009). The evaluation included repeated assessments using the ECERS-R and the PAS. Baseline Average PAS Item Scores ranged from 2.14 to 5.59. On average, programs had more than seven items scoring 2.00 or less.

The results of the study found that both individualized support through on-site consultation and group support through workshops and network meetings contributed to quality improvements, but in different ways. Individualized consultation contributed to greater improvements in the program's classroom learning environments, as measured by the ECERS-R. Group support was strongly associated with improvement in program administration and operations, as measured by the PAS. When examined together in a multiple regression analysis, both types of support were associated with decreased variability in the quality of the classrooms.

On average, programs improved their PAS scores by 2 or more points on just over six items. The researchers state that just as important as the improvements in specific areas of administration were changes in directors' understanding of their own leadership role. They became better organized and more focused, recognizing areas of administrative practice they needed to work on.

Multiple regressions that controlled for the initial PAS score and included the hours per month that the staff participated in professional development workshops and director meetings were statistically significant in predicting change in PAS scores and in the number of PAS items scored as high, explaining 60% and 58% respectively of the variance in these measures of program improvement.

Additionally, the teaching staff's participation in professional development was strongly associated with improvements in their center's PAS scores. The study concludes that as directors gain greater understanding of their leadership and managerial roles in supervision and quality improvement, they take advantage of more professional development opportunities for their staff.

Study #12. A final evaluation report was conducted by the Policy Equity Group of the Early Learning Ventures (ELV) Early Head Start-Child Care (EHS-CC) partnership model in Colorado (Etter & Capizzano, 2017). This evaluation study is particularly interesting because of the comprehensive methodology used to test the impact of a shared services alliance on the quality of early care and education programs. Early Learning Ventures is a unique EHS-CC Partnership in that it is designed as a shared services model that supports a statewide network of child care programs. The shared services model consists of business supports for data management, child recruitment, and financial practices; leadership development for program administrators; coaching and professional development for the teaching staff; and family and community engagement.

The evaluation was conducted to document successes and challenges and assess the shared service model's impact on improving program quality. Baseline data were collected in late 2015 using multiple measures: the Head Start Monitoring Protocol, the PAS, the Business Administration Scale for Family Child Care (BAS), the Early Childhood Job Satisfaction Scale (ECJSS), the ECWES, the Classroom Assessment Scoring System (CLASS), and the Family

Strengths, Needs, and Interests Survey (SNIS). Follow-up data were collected approximately 10 months later. Over this relatively short period of time there were significant improvements on several important indicators of business capacity and program quality.

The sample was comprised of 77 teaching and administrative staff working in 17 center-based programs across four counties in Colorado. Programs made significant improvement in their overall Average PAS Scores from baseline to follow-up, with a very large effect size ($d = 2.07$). At baseline, the centers averaged a score of 2.46, falling below the threshold score of 3.0, which is considered a *minimal* level of quality. At follow-up, the centers averaged a score of 3.85, which is a significant increase (pretest $M = 2.46$, posttest $M = 3.85$, $t = -9.51$, $p < .001$). The overall Average PAS Score for ELV programs was significantly lower than the national sample ($M = 3.47$) at baseline. By follow-up, ELV programs had closed the gap and had scores that mirrored the norm sample. These results suggest a significant improvement in business and professional practices for center-based programs after participating in the first year of the ELV intervention.

Looking at individual PAS Item Scores, there were significant changes in 19 of the 25 items from baseline to follow-up. There was a very large effect size on improvements to Staff Orientation ($d = 1.71$), Facilities Management ($d = 1.05$), Internal Communications ($d = 1.11$), Family Communications ($d = 1.93$), Family Support and Involvement ($d = 1.68$), External Communications ($d = 1.31$), Community Outreach ($d = 2.03$), and Use of Technology ($d = 1.33$).

Overall, ELV programs made significant gains across the PAS in terms of progress from baseline to follow-up and closed gaps in areas in which they started out below the norm sample averages. The notable exceptions to the global improvements achieved on the PAS were in the areas of Staff Benefits and Staff Qualifications, suggesting these are areas of administration needing a longer-term intervention and greater public investment to demonstrate significant improvements.

Study #13. This study (Yaya-Bryson, Scott-Little, Akman, & Cassidy, 2020) examined the quality of early childhood education programs in two different quality rating and improvement contexts, one in Turkey and the other in North Carolina. The ECERS-R was used to evaluate the quality of the classrooms, and the PAS was used to evaluate the quality of administrative practices. The sample consisted of a total of 40 early childhood programs, half located in Turkey and half located in North Carolina. International reports indicate that different countries have different cultural contexts, approaches, and policies regarding early childhood education (ECE) systems of quality improvement. However, there are scant comparative international ECE studies that report data collected at the individual program level. This comparative international study is important because of its focus on the administrative quality of ECE programs.

Pilot studies were conducted prior to collecting data with the PAS. Co-raters selected to collect data with the ECERS-R in Turkey were also trained to administer the PAS using the translated version. The primary researcher and three other trained raters administered the PAS for the pilot in Turkey. Inter-rater reliability for the Turkish co-raters was calculated as .98. In North Carolina, the primary researcher and a reliable PAS assessor conducted assessments in a pilot study. Inter-rater reliability for the PAS was computed as .92.

For the total PAS scores on the quality of administrative practices, the t-test comparison between Turkey ($M = 3.5$, $SD = .94$) and North Carolina ($M = 3.3$, $SD = .95$) was not significant, $t = .467$, $p = .643$. Mean scores for Turkey and North Carolina on each PAS subscale fell within a low to medium range (1 is *inadequate* to 7 is *excellent*). There were no significant differences between national contexts on any of the PAS subscales.

An additional purpose of the study was to explore the associations in the overall ratings of classroom environment quality and administrative quality in each quality improvement system. Pearson correlations were used to evaluate the strength of the relationship between overall ECERS-R score and overall PAS score in each system. In Turkey, there was a significant correlation between ECERS-R and PAS overall scores of .73, $p = .000$. In North Carolina, there was also a significant correlation between ECERS-R and PAS overall scores of .69, $p = .001$. These correlations indicated that ratings of classroom environment quality were strongly associated with the quality of administrative practices in each system.

Results from this study suggest that it may be important for quality improvement systems in different national contexts to assess administrative practices as well as classroom quality. Standards for administrative practices should first be established, and measures such as the PAS should be included in the program quality evaluation system.

Study #14. A 20-year evaluation of a leadership development model, Taking Charge of Change™ (TCC), was conducted to discern the impact of training on directors' perceptions of competence and on the quality of organizational practices at their centers. The researchers (Talan, Bloom, & Kelton, 2014) also looked at the current job status, career decisions, and professional achievements of the 502 alumni since completing the leadership academy.

Pre- and post-data from the twenty cohorts of directors who completed TCC included the Training Needs Assessment Survey (TNAS), measuring perceived competence in different knowledge and skill areas; the PAS, measuring the quality of leadership and management practices at participants' centers; and the ECWES, assessing the work climate of their organizations. An additional survey was completed by alumni of TCC to learn about their current work status, leadership journey, and any professional accomplishments.

The PAS was first published in 2004 to measure and improve the quality of administrative practices in center-based early learning programs. For the current study, five of the 25 items were used. The 18 indicator strands comprising the five items relate to the focus of the

TCC curriculum (e.g., Item 1: Staff Orientation, Item 2: Supervision and Performance Appraisal, Item 3: Staff Development, Item 9: Internal Communications, Item 16: Family Communications). Pre- and post-PAS assessments were conducted for TCC participants beginning in 2007 (Cohort #15). The assessments were done by a reliable PAS assessor who was not involved in the TCC training. Each assessment included a brief tour of the facility, an interview with the administrator, and a review of documentation. Seventy-four programs were included in the PAS data analysis for this study.

The results of the data analysis revealed an increase in scores in all five items between the pre- and post-administration of the PAS. Statistically significant differences were found in three of the items: staff orientation (pretest $M = 2.81$, posttest $M = 3.75$, $t = 2.57$, $p < .05$), staff development (pretest $M = 3.32$, posttest $M = 4.21$, $t = 2.54$, $p < .01$), and family communications (pretest $M = 2.81$, posttest $M = 4.07$, $t = 3.47$, $p < .001$). When comparing the average PAS item scores to the national averages for similar early childhood programs, the quality of leadership and management practices in TCC participants' programs was lower than the national average at the beginning of the training. By the end of the training, the mean item scores were higher than the national average in four out of the five items assessed.

Overall, the results of the study suggest that participation in the TCC model is associated with positive personal and program outcomes, indicating that effective leadership development for directors of center-based early childhood programs should be systematic, intensive, and relevant.

Study #15. The Mentoring Pairs for Child Care (MPCC) was a director training program funded by the government of Ontario, Canada, as part of a strategy to enhance the quality of the child care programs throughout the province. One of the study's three research questions was to determine whether graduation from MPCC enhanced the administrative practices of directors.

The program design was informed by two existing initiatives: the Taking Charge of Change leadership development model implemented by the McCormick Center for Early Childhood Leadership and the Partners in Practice Mentoring Model, field-tested with experienced directors mentoring newer directors. Unique to MPCC was the use of occupational standards for center administrators as the foundation for its curriculum and its emphasis on collegial mentoring.

The sample for this study (Doherty, Ferguson, Ressler, & Lomotey, 2015) consisted of 403 current directors or assistant directors drawn from all 28 areas of Ontario. Only 340 participants completed the year-long program, reflecting an attrition rate of 15.6%. Participants with less than five years of director experience were matched with more experienced directors from their geographic areas. A subsample of the 28 participating areas was selected to provide centers with on-site pre- and post-training assessments of quality. The final number of observed programs (57) comprised 14% of the entire sample.

Data were collected by ten reliable assessors using the ECERS-R and the PAS. The study found significantly higher post-MPCC scores on the total PAS (pretest $M = 2.8$, posttest $M = 3.3$, $t = 4.31$, $p < .001$) and on seven of the nine subscales assessed. (The Staff Qualifications subscale was not assessed due to difficulty converting American higher education terminology to that used in Canada.) The effect size for the total PAS score was $d = .57$, $p < .001$, indicating that MPCC had a moderate impact on administrative quality. Considering that posttest data had to be collected within two months of completion of the MPCC program, the impact of the training model on the administrative quality of directors' centers was notable.

The most significant PAS changes were demonstrated in the subscales where directors had the greatest agency: Human Resources Development (pretest $M = 2.4$, posttest $M = 3.1$, $t = 4.07$, $p < .001$), Marketing and Public Relations (pretest $M = 3.2$, posttest $M = 4.1$, $t = 4.96$, $p < .01$), and Use of Technology (pretest $M = 4.1$, posttest $M = 4.5$, $t = 2.81$, $p < .01$). In the subscales comprised of administrative

areas in which directors need additional approvals or funds, Child Assessment and Personnel Cost and Allocation, the change in scores was not significant. Finally, the study found significant positive correlation ($r = .48$, $p < .01$) between administrative and global classroom quality as measured by the ECERS-R.

Study #16. The Head Start Designation Renewal System (DRS) was created in 2011 as an accountability system to determine whether Head Start grantees were delivering high-quality services and to implement a competitive grant-making process where high-quality services were found to be lacking. In 2016, the results of a study evaluating the early implementation of DRS was released. Researchers from the Urban Institute and Frank Porter Graham Child Development Institute (Derrick-Mills et al., 2016) evaluated the DRS using a mixed-methods design that integrated administrative data and secondary data sources, observational assessments, and interviews to discern the multiple dimensions of comprehensive program quality.

A stratified random sample of 71 grantees (35 designated for competition and 36 not designated) was recruited. The reason for designation included deficiencies in compliance with Head Start performance standards (40%) and low CLASS scores (69%). Within grantees, there were 554 classrooms serving preschool children.

One research question examined whether the DRS differentiates higher- versus lower-quality programs. Quality measures aligned with the two DRS conditions that account for over 99% of designations (deficiencies in meeting performance standards and low CLASS scores) were selected to answer this question. Analyses tested for mean differences in quality ratings at the grantee level. The PAS was used to assess program quality constructs in the following areas: Family and Community Engagement; Child Development & Education; Management, Operations & Governance Systems; Fiscal Integrity & Vulnerability; and Classroom Quality.

The evaluation study found that overall classroom and center quality of grantees designated for competition for any reason was not significantly different from the quality of not-designated grantees, but the quality of overall center operations was significantly lower in grantees designated for deficiencies than in not-designated grantees. Among grantees designated for deficiencies, the PAS subscales measuring the quality of staff qualifications, personnel costs and allocation, and fiscal management were rated significantly lower than for not-designated grantees. It should be noted, however, that the analyses of the PAS data involved multiple imputations to account for missing data.

In Sum

The results of the sixteen studies briefly described in the preceding section provide compelling evidence that the PAS is a reliable, valid instrument that approaches early childhood program quality from a different perspective than assessments focusing exclusively on the classroom learning environment or teacher-child interactions. The consensus appears to be that multiple measures generate a more comprehensive and refined picture of the overall program quality. The *Program Administration Scale* is particularly useful in highlighting organizational strengths, pinpointing areas in need of improvement, and guiding administrators in making incremental changes that benefit staff, families, and children.

References and Resources

Abel, M., Talan, T., & Masterson, M. (2017). Whole leadership: A framework for early childhood programs. *Exchange 39*(233): 22–25.

Arend, L. (2010, October). *Filling the void: A call for educational administration preparation specific to early childhood leaders.* Paper presented at the Annual Conference of the University Council for Educational Administration, New Orleans, LA.

Arnett, J. (1989). Caregivers in day care centers: Does training matter? *Journal of Applied Developmental Psychology, 10*(4), 541–552.

Aubrey, C., Godfrey, R., & Harris, A. (2012). How do they manage? An investigation of early childhood leadership. *Educational Management Administration & Leadership, 41*(1), 5–29.

Barnett, W. S. (2003a, March). *Better teachers, better preschools: Student achievement linked to teacher qualifications* (Issue 2). National Institute for Early Education Research.

Barnett, W. S. (2003b, May). *Low wages = low quality: Solving the real preschool teacher crisis* (Issue 3). National Institute for Early Education Research.

Bassok, D., Bellows, L., Markowitz, A. J., & Sadowski, K. C. (2021). New evidence on teacher turnover in early childhood. *Educational Evaluation and Policy Analysis, 43*(1), 172–180.

Bella, J. (2008, July/August). Improving leadership and management practices: One step at a time. *Exchange*, 6–10.

Bella, J., & Bloom, P. J. (2003). *Zoom: The impact of early childhood leadership training on role perceptions, job performance, and career decisions.* McCormick Center for Early Childhood Leadership, National Louis University.

Bertachi, J. (1996, October/November). Relationship-based organizations. *Zero to Three Bulletin, 17*(2), 2–7.

Bloom, P. J. (1996). The quality of work life in NAEYC accredited and non-accredited early childhood programs. *Early Education and Development, 7*(4), 301–317.

Bloom, P. J. (2004). Leadership as a way of thinking. *Zero to Three, 25*(2), 21–26.

Bloom, P. J. (2011). *Circle of influence: Implementing shared decision making and participative management* (2nd ed.). Lake Forest, IL: New Horizons.

Bloom, P. J. (2016). *Measuring work attitudes in the early childhood setting: Technical manual for the Early Childhood Job Satisfaction Survey and the Early Childhood Work Environment Survey* (3rd ed.). McCormick Center for Early Childhood Leadership, National Louis University.

Bloom, P. J., & Abel, M. (2015). Expanding the lens—Leadership as an organizational asset. *Young Children, 70*(2), 8–13.

Bloom, P. J., Hentschel, A., & Bella, J. (2013). *Inspiring peak performance: Competence, commitment, and collaboration.* New Horizons.

Bloom, P. J., & Talan, T. N. (2006, October). *Changes in program quality associated with participation in a professional development initiative*. McCormick Center for Early Childhood Leadership, National Louis University.

Caven, M., Khanani, M., Zhang, X., & Parker, C. E. (2021). *Center- and program-level factors associated with turnover in the early childhood education workforce* (REL 2021-069). U.S. Department of Education, Institute of Education Sciences, National Center for Education Evaluation and Regional Assistance, Regional Educational Laboratory Northeast & Islands.

Center for the Study of Child Care Employment & American Federation of Teachers Educational Foundation. (2019). *Model work standards for teaching staff in center-based child care.* Center for the Study of Child Care Employment, University of California, Berkeley. American Federation of Teachers Educational Foundation.

Cochran, M. (2007). Caregiver and teacher compensation. *Zero to Three, 28*(1), 42–47.

Cornille, T., Mullis, R., Mullis, A., & Shriner, M. (2006). An examination of child care teachers in for-profit and nonprofit child care centers. *Early Child Development and Care, 176*(6), 631–641.

Cost, Quality, and Child Outcomes Study Team. (1995). *Cost, quality, and child outcomes in child care centers.* Department of Economics, University of Colorado at Denver.

Culkin, M. L. (2000). *Managing quality in young children's programs: The leader's role.* Teachers College Press.

Dennis, S., & O'Connor, E. (2013). Reexamining quality in early childhood education: Exploring the relationship between the organizational climate and the classroom. *Journal of Research in Childhood Education 27*(1), 74–92.

Derrick-Mills, T. Burchinal, M., Peters, H. E., De Marco, A., Forestieri, N., Fyffe, S., Hanson, D., Heller, C., Pratt, E., Sandstrom, H., Triplett, T., & Woods, T. (2016). *Early Implementation of the Head Start Designation Renewal System: Volume I.* OPRE Report #: 2016-75a. Office of Planning, Research and Evaluation, Administration for Children and Families, U.S. Department of Health and Human Services.

Division for Early Childhood. (2014). *DEC recommended practices in early intervention/early childhood special education 2014.* http://www.dec-sped.org/recommendedpractices

Doherty, G., Ferguson, T. M., Ressler, G., & Lomotey, J. (2015). Enhancing child care quality by director training and collegial mentoring. *Early Childhood Research and Practice 17*(1), 1–11.

Douglass, A. (2017). *Leading for change in early care and education: Cultivating leadership from within.* Teachers College Press.

Douglass, A. (2018). Redefining leadership: Lessons from an early education leadership development initiative. *Early Childhood Education Journal, 46,* 387–396.

Etter, K., & Capizzano, J. (2016, June). *Early Learning Ventures Early Head Start-Child Care Partnership Model.* Washington, DC: Policy Equity Group.

Gittell, J. (2016). *Transforming relationships for high performance: The power of relational coordination.* Stanford, CA: Stanford University Press.

Halle, T., Vick Whittaker, J. E., & Anderson, R. (2010). *Quality in early childhood care and education settings: A compendium of measures* (2nd ed.). Child Trends.

Harms, T., Clifford, R., & Cryer, D. (2005). *Early Childhood Environment Rating Scale–Revised.* Teachers College Press.

Herzenberg, S., Price, M., & Bradley, D. (2005). *Losing ground in early childhood education: Declining workforce qualifications in an expanding industry, 1979–2004.* Keystone Research Center.

Hewett, B., & La Paro, K. M. (2020). Organizational climate: Collegiality and supervisor support in early childhood education programs. *Early Childhood Education Journal, 48,* 415–427.

High/Scope Educational Research Foundation. (2019). *Preschool Program Quality Assessment-Revised.* https://highscope .org/wp-content/uploads/2019/08/PQA-R-Manual-8.28.19.pdf

Hujala, E., Eskelinen, M., Keskinen, S., Chen, C., Inoue, C., Matsumoto, M., & Kawase, M. (2016). Leadership tasks in early childhood education in Finland, Japan, and Singapore. *Journal of Research in Childhood Education 30*(3), 406–421.

Institute of Medicine & National Research Council. (2015). *Transforming the workforce for children birth through age 8: A unifying foundation.* National Academies Press.

Kagan, S. L., & Bowman, B. (Eds.). (1997). *Leadership in early care and education.* National Association for the Education of Young Children.

Kagan, S. L., Brooks-Gunn, J., Westheimer, M., Tarrant, K., Cortazar, A., Johnson, A., Philipsen, N., & Pressman, A. (2008). *New York City early care and education unified performance measurement system: A pilot study.* National Center for Children and Families.

Kagan, S. L., Kauerz, K., & Tarrant, K. (2008). *The early care and education teaching workforce at the fulcrum: An agenda for reform.* Teachers College Press.

Kangas, J., Venninen, T., & Ojala, M. (2015). Distributed leadership as administrative practice in Finnish early childhood education and care. *Educational Management, Administration & Leadership, 44*(4), 617–631.

King, E. K., Johnson, A., Cassidy, D., Wang, Y., Lower, J., & Kintner-Duffy, V. (2015, October). Preschool teachers' financial well-being and work time supports: Associations with children's emotional expressions and behaviors in classrooms. *Early Childhood Education Journal, 44*(6), 545–553.

Kirby, G., Douglass, A., Lyskawa, J., Jones, C., & Malone, L. (2021). *Understanding leadership in early care and education: A literature review.* OPRE Report 2021-02. Office of Planning, Research, and Evaluation, Administration for Children and Families, U.S. Department of Health and Human Services

Lower, J. K., & Cassidy, D. J. (2007, Winter). Child care work environments: The relationship with learning environments. *Journal of Research in Childhood Education, 22*(2), 189–204.

McCormick Center for Early Childhood Leadership. (2007, Spring). Program characteristics associated with utilization of early childhood professional development funding. *Research Notes.* National Louis University.

McCormick Center for Early Childhood Leadership. (2010a). Connecting the dots: Director qualifications, instructional leadership practices, and learning environments in early childhood programs. *Research Notes.* National Louis University.

McCormick Center for Early Childhood Leadership. (2010b). Head Start administrative practices, director qualifications, and links to classroom quality. *Research Notes.* National Louis University.

McCormick Center for Early Childhood Leadership. (2021, Summer). A window on early childhood administrative practices: 2010–2021. *Research Notes*. National Louis University.

McKelvey, L., Chapin-Critz, M., Johnson, B., Bokony, P., Conners-Burrow, N., & Whiteside-Mansell, L. (2010). *Better Beginnings: Evaluating Arkansas' path to better child outcomes*. Partners for Inclusive Communities.

Means, K. M. & Pepper, A. (2010). *Best practices of accreditation facilitation projects: A framework for program improvement using NAEYC early childhood program standards and accreditation criteria*. National Association for the Education of Young Children.

Mietlicki, C. (2010, October). *Tennessee Early Childhood Program Administrator Credential: Year two evaluation report*. Tennessee Early Childhood Training Alliance, Tennessee State University.

Miller, J. A., & Bogatova, T. (2007). *Early care and education workforce development initiatives: Program design, implementation, and outcomes*. KeyStone Research Corporation.

Minkos, M., Sassu, K., Gregory, J., Patwa, S. S., Theodore, L., & Femc-Bagwell, M. (2017). Culturally responsive practice and the role of school administrators. *Psychology in the Schools 54*(10), 1260–1266.

National Association for the Education of Young Children. (2019a). *NAEYC early learning program accreditation standards and assessment items*. https://www.naeyc.org/sites/default/files/globally-shared/downloads/PDFs/accreditation/early-learning/standards_assessment_2019.pdf

National Association for the Education of Young Children. (2019b). *Professional standards and competencies for early childhood educators*. https://www.naeyc.org/resources/position-statements/professional-standards-competencies

National Association for the Education of Young Children. (2022). *Developmentally appropriate practice in early childhood programs serving children from birth through age 8* (4th ed.). National Association for the Education of Young Children.

Phillips, D., Mekos, D., Scarr, S., McCartney, K., & Abbott-Shim, M. (2000). Within and beyond the classroom door: Assessing quality in child care centers. *Early Childhood Research Quarterly, 15*(4), 475–496.

Rohacek, M., Adams, G., & Kisker, E. (2010). *Understanding quality in context: Child care centers, communities, markets, and public policy*. Urban Institute.

Rous, B., Grove, J., Cox, M., Townley, K., & Crumpton, G. (2008). *The impact of the Kentucky professional development framework on child care, Head Start, and preschool classroom quality and child outcomes*. Human Development Institute, University of Kentucky.

Sabol, T. J., Sommer, T. E., Sanchez, A., & Busby, A. K. (2018). A new approach to defining and measuring family engagement in early childhood education programs. *AERA Open*. July 2018. doi:10.1177/2332858418785904

Stephens, S. A. (2009, August). *Quality New York: Assessment of its contributions to program improvement in early care and education programs in New York City*. Center for Assessment and Policy Development. https://static1.squarespace.com/static/536ce727e4b0a03c478b38e4/t/557738b2e4b0a44e2a8ea545/1433876658414/Quality+New+York-+Assessment+of+Its+Contributions+to+Program+Improvement+in+Early+Care+and+Education+Programs+in+New+York+City.pdf

Talan, T. N. (2007). *Roots and wings: Portrait of an early childhood learning organization* (Doctoral dissertation). National Louis University.

Talan, T. N. (2010, May/June). Distributive leadership: Something new or something borrowed? *Exchange*. http://www .childcareexchange.com/article/distributed-leadership -something-new-or-something-borrowed/5019308/

Talan, T. N., Bloom, P. J., & Kelton, R. (2014). Building the leadership capacity of early childhood directors: An evaluation of a leadership development model. *Early Childhood Research and Practice 16*(1 and 2), 3–8.

Torquati, J.C., Raikes, H., & Huddleston-Casas, C. A. (2007). Teacher education, motivation, compensation, workplace support, and links to quality of center-based child care and teachers' intention to stay in the early childhood profession. *Early Childhood Research Quarterly, 22*(2), 261–275.

Vu, J., Jeon, H., & Howes, C. (2008). Formal education, credential, or both: Early childhood program classroom practices. *Early Education and Development, 19*(3), 479–504.

Whalen, S.P., Horsley, H. L., Parkinson, K. K., & Pacchiano, D. (2016). A development evaluation study of a professional development initiative to strengthen organizational conditions in early education settings. *Journal of Applied Research on Children: Informing Policy for Children at Risk, 7*(2).

Whitebook, M., McLean, C., & Austin, L. (2016). *Early childhood workforce index*. Institute for Research on Labor and Employment, University of California, Berkeley.

Whitebook, M., Phillips, D., & Howes, C. (2014). *Worthy work, STILL unlivable wages: The early childhood workforce 25 years after the National Child Care Staffing Study*. Center for the Study of Child Care Employment, University of California, Berkeley.

Whitebook, M., Ryan, S., Kipnis, F., & Sakai, L. (2008, February). *Partnering for preschool: A study of center directors in New Jersey's mixed-delivery Abbott Program*. Center for the Study of Child Care Employment, Institute for Research on Labor and Employment, University of California at Berkeley.

Yaya-Bryson, D., Scott-Little, C., Akman, B., & Cassidy, D. (2020). A comparison of early childhood classroom environments and program administrative quality in Turkey and North Carolina. *International Journal of Early Childhood, 52*, 233–248.

Zeng, S., Douglass, A., Lee, Y., & DelVecchio, B. (2020). Preliminary efficacy and feasibility of a business leadership training program for small child care providers. *Early Childhood Education Journal, 49*, 27–36.

Zinsser, K., Denham, S., Curby, T., & Chazan-Cohen, R. (2016). Early childhood directors as socializers of emotional climate. *Learning Environment Research 19*(2), 267–290.

Notes

Notes

Notes

Notes

Notes

Notes

Notes